Writing for Rights

Writing for Rights

BY

PATRICE W. GLENN
Alabama State University

United Kingdom – North America – Japan – India – Malaysia – China

Emerald Publishing Limited
Emerald Publishing, Floor 5, Northspring, 21-23 Wellington Street, Leeds LS1 4DL

First edition 2025

Editorial matter and selection © 2025 Patrice W. Glenn

Published under exclusive licence by Emerald Publishing Limited.
Reprints and permissions service

Contact: www.copyright.com

No part of this book may be reproduced, stored in a retrieval system, transmitted in any form or by any means electronic, mechanical, photocopying, recording or otherwise without either the prior written permission of the publisher or a licence permitting restricted copying issued in the UK by The Copyright Licensing Agency and in the USA by The Copyright Clearance Center. Any opinions expressed in the chapters are those of the authors. Whilst Emerald makes every effort to ensure the quality and accuracy of its content, Emerald makes no representation implied or otherwise, as to the chapters' suitability and application and disclaims any warranties, express or implied, to their use.

British Library Cataloguing in Publication Data

A catalogue record for this book is available from the British Library

ISBNs:
978-1-83708-490-6   HB
978-1-83708-491-3   PB
978-1-83708-492-0   EPDF
978-1-83708-493-7   EPUB

CONTENTS

	From the Author	vii
1.	Focus on Learning	1
2.	Fighting to be Heard	3
3.	Your Voice in Communication	5
4.	Writing for Your Audience	11
5.	Getting Organized	13
6.	Taking "Note" of Information Around You	17
7.	Study Methods for Growth	21
8.	Critical Thinking in Pursuit of Social Justice	23
9.	The Writing We Know Best	27
10.	Transitioning to College-Level Writing: Embracing Diversity and Social Justice	29
11.	Elements of Rhetoric: Crafting Language for Social Justice	33
12.	Types of Writing	35
13.	The Journey of Advocacy Through Writing	45
14.	The Crucible of Justice: Writing to Advocate Through Facts, Emotion, Ethics, and Logic	49
15.	The Power of Prewriting	53
16.	Harnessing the Power of Outlining	59
17.	Empowering Voices Through the Draft	63
18.	Benefits of a Break	71

19. Ready to Revise 77
20. Empowering Through Precise Proofreading 83
21. Parts of Speech 87
22. Nouns 91
23. Common and Proper Nouns 95
24. Verbs 99
25. Sentence Basics 107
26. Making Subjects and Verbs Agree 113
27. Punctuating Sentences 117
28. Adjectives and Adverbs 121
29. Pronoun and Antecedent Agreement 127
30. Commonly Confused Words 133
31. Transitions 139
32. Double Negatives 143
33. Sentence Variety 147
34. Quality Content 151
35. Using Numbers 157
36. The Profound Process of Publishing 159
37. A Change in Our Writing 161
    Author Biography 165

FROM THE AUTHOR

One of the lasting memories from the year 2020 will undoubtedly be the protests sparked by the deaths of George Floyd and others at the hands of police. Throughout that year, incidents of excessive force and police brutality were heavily scrutinized, leaving a lasting impression on us all.

Alongside the protests, the COVID-19 pandemic and its resulting lockdowns dominated headlines and discussions. The effects of the pandemic will likely be discussed and studied for years to come, possibly overshadowing the social justice issues that also arose during the year.

Death, in its many forms, became a universal subject in 2020. Whether it was the loss of lives due to a microscopic virus or the killing of a loved one, the topic was real, immediate, and threatening. While these tragedies caught our attention for a time, unfortunately, the discussion often fades, and the names of victims like Ahmaud Arbrey, George Floyd, and Breonna Taylor are forgotten.

Furthermore, in 2020, there was a notable increase in violence against Black and Latinx individuals in the LGBTQ+ communities. The initial surge of outrage over these injustices often subsided, replaced by new incidents and forms of discrimination. Perhaps our emotions waned because we knew that something else would soon take its place—a new killing, a new injustice, a new senseless death.

Writing for Rights, pages vii–viii.
Copyright © 2025 *Patrice W. Glenn*
Published under exclusive licence by Emerald Publishing Limited
ISBNs: 978-1-83708-490-6 HB, 978-1-83708-491-3 PB,
978-1-83708-492-0 EPDF, 978-1-83708-493-7 EPUB

Yet, despite the ever-changing news cycle, the pursuit of social justice and fair solutions continues for many advocates. These people tirelessly protest and express their frustrations and passions, often through writing. As E.L. Doctorow noted, "Good writing is supposed to evoke sensation in the reader—not the fact that it is raining, but the feeling of being rained upon."

In writing this book, my hope is to demonstrate the power of words. Writing is not just a means of expression; it's a tool to communicate frustration, passion, and drive change. I hope this book helps you find your voice and use it to impact the communities and groups you care about, allowing you to be part of the ongoing conversation and movement towards justice.

CHAPTER 1

FOCUS ON LEARNING

Sometimes, I wish I could rid all classes of grades to create a more just and equitable learning environment. In a world committed to social justice, removing grades would alleviate the pressure on students from marginalized communities, who often face additional stress and societal expectations to earn an A, a B, or settle for a C. The problem, compounded by systemic inequalities in our world, is that many students are driven to complete their assignments primarily by grades. This system perpetuates the idea that a simple letter grade determines the value of education, ignoring the diverse backgrounds and learning needs of students.

However, education is a universal right, taking place everywhere, and its value transcends mere monetary measurements: composition book-$1.99; 10-pack of blue ink pens—$4.95; mathematics book-$75.00; education—priceless. As Anatole France, the French author, wisely said, "An education isn't how much you have committed to memory, or even how much you know. It's being able to differentiate between what you do know and what you don't."

Nevertheless, in a world fraught with disparities, many learners do not enter classes with their energy focused on genuine learning. For some, driven by societal pressures and inequalities, earning a "good grade" becomes the sole focus. To build an educational system centered on justice and equality, we must challenge this way of thinking. We must focus on learning and make "earning" secondary.

Writing for Rights, pages 1–2.
Copyright © 2025 *Patrice W. Glenn*
Published under exclusive licence by Emerald Publishing Limited
ISBNs: 978-1-83708-490-6 HB, 978-1-83708-491-3 PB,
978-1-83708-492-0 EPDF, 978-1-83708-493-7 EPUB

This is particularly true for foundation courses, the classes that establish skills that the learner will use throughout their education. These foundation courses, such as basic writing, should be accessible and inclusive to all, reflecting the diverse backgrounds and needs of the learners.

CHALLENGE—Embrace a commitment to social justice in education, focusing on the same energy and spirit of survival that has brought you to this point. Think about creating a learning environment that is compassionate, fair, and inclusive, not just for a minute, but as a lasting legacy. Think about it just a minute.

Thinking?

Now, harness that energy and use it to propel yourself through this educational process. Enjoy the process; focus on learning, not earning. You can do it!

Are you ready?

HOW TO USE THIS TEXT

Some books are novels that we read in sequential order. We experience them with emotion and engagement. This is not one of those books. This text is a resource for you to reference as needed. The content presented is not meant to be linear although that information is presented in a logical linear fashion. Therefore, it may prove best for you to jump around from one chapter to one that precedes it. Additionally, if you are like me, you may need to double check your thoughts. In such a case, I pick up text resources, flip to the information I seek, and verify my information or correct my misinformation. For all intents and purposes, this is how you should use this text.

You may also be guided through this text by a teacher or instructor. He or she knows best, so follow the direction provided.

CHAPTER 2

FIGHTING TO BE HEARD

> I am no longer accepting the things I cannot change. I am changing the things I cannot accept.
>
> —*Angela Davis*

No matter your background or where you come from, you may have felt ignored and overlooked at times. Perhaps you've witnessed police brutality against people who resemble you or seen those in power remain silent in the face of anti-LGBTQ+ harassment or bias.

These experiences can foster fear and anxiety, impacting your sense of safety, belonging, and overall well-being. Likewise, those who suffer such injustices may feel isolated and forsaken. Have you ever felt this way?

It's common to feel despair when faced with massive injustice. Sometimes, you might think that there's nothing you can say or do to improve the situation. Even worse, you may fear that your efforts or words will be disregarded simply because of who you are. This feeling, often referred to as "voicelessness," is familiar to many, especially those from marginalized or underrepresented groups. At our core, we all want our experiences and concerns to be recognized and heard. I know I do.

4 • WRITING FOR RIGHTS

Maybe you've wanted to stand up against issues like gender inequality, homophobia, or racial injustice, but were unsure how to proceed. It's understandable. As Elie Wiesel once said, "There may be times when we are powerless to prevent injustice, but there must never be a time when we fail to protest." In this chapter, I use the terms "fight" and "protest" interchangeably to mean active objection. Regardless of the social issue that bothers you, you have the power to take action.

Not every act of protest or fight needs to be grand or public. Some of the most powerful and essential actions are small and communicated within small circles. These efforts can create a ripple effect that expands into larger groups. But to make a difference, we must first take a stand.

In his speech at the 2006 groundbreaking of the Dr. Martin Luther King, Jr. National Memorial, President Barack Obama stated, "Through words, he gave voice to the voiceless. Through deeds, he gave courage to the faint of heart." Your words for social justice can take many forms, including writing opinion pieces, letters to politicians, policy recommendations, personal narratives, academic research, or creative works like poetry and fiction. You might also speak at public events. The power of our "words for social justice" is in the message, and at the core of those messages is your determination to fight.

> Unless someone like you cares a whole awful lot, nothing is going to get better. It's not.
> —*Dr. Seuss,* The Lorax

CHAPTER 3

YOUR VOICE IN COMMUNICATION

All speech, written or spoken, is a dead language, until it finds a willing and prepared hearer.

—*Robert Louis Stevenson [Scottish poet]*

THE IMPACT OF STANDARDIZED COMMUNICATION IN PURSUIT OF SOCIAL JUSTICE

In the U.S., communication's value often rests on the receiver's perceptions, subtly reinforcing social hierarchies. For instance, when someone uses standard American English, they may be perceived as intelligent and taken seriously. In contrast, those who speak differently might be unfairly viewed as less capable. This unjust bias is not just a matter of personal opinion; it's deeply interwoven into our social fabric, influencing employment, education, and even political advocacy.

It might be easy to dismiss how others view your communication style, but this attitude overlooks an essential truth: We don't live isolated from each other; we coexist and rely on one another. How we communicate, and how we're perceived, impacts our ability to evoke change. It can make a difference in a job interview, a promotion, or even a political debate, such as the rising cost of education.

Recognizing and embracing this importance of communication isn't just about personal gain. It's about empowering ourselves and others to promote social justice causes effectively. Embracing standard American English in the U.S. is not just a tool for personal advancement but a means to advocate for positive change.

A BRIEF HISTORY OF THE ENGLISH LANGUAGE

Understanding the history of the English language can help us comprehend the roots of these biases. Originating from West Germanic language and evolving through influences from Latin, French, and various dialects, English has undergone significant changes over centuries.

By the late 1300s, English became the judicial system's official language, solidifying its status. With the creation of standard American English in the 19th century, language became more than just a means of communication; it became a way to divide or unite people.

> The way we communicate with others and ourselves ultimately determines the quality of our lives.
> —*Anthony Robbins (American advisor to leaders)*

RECOGNIZING AND ADDRESSING COMMUNICATION ERRORS

While standard American English has become the norm, many people naturally speak with variations. Some examples of these variations are:

1. Use of "ain't": *She ain't my friend.*
2. Dropping the "g" in "ing": *Where are we goin'?*
3. Using "gonna" instead of "going to": *The event is gonna be exciting.*

Though these might be considered "errors," it's important to recognize that they are part of our diverse linguistic heritage.

IMPROVING VERBAL COMMUNICATION

Improving communication doesn't mean abandoning our unique voices but expanding our ability to communicate with different audiences. Some ways to achieve this include:

Listening to ourselves and standard American English speakers.

- Identifying strengths and weaknesses.
- Practicing daily.

- Improving our speech doesn't just make us more articulate; it enhances our ability to advocate for justice and equality.

SPEAKING, WRITING, AND SOCIAL CHANGE

Writing is equally vital, often providing the first impression of us. Clear, effective writing can open doors and opportunities. Improving speech naturally leads to better writing, empowering us to use various forms of writing to promote social change.

CHARACTERISTICS OF AN EFFECTIVE COMPOSITION

An effective composition, whether aiming to persuade or entertain, must have:

- Clear grammar and sentence structure,
- A sense of purpose and organization, and
- An engaging style appropriate for the audience.

These characteristics enable us to reach our audience more effectively, supporting our pursuit of social justice.

COMMUNICATION FOR SOCIAL JUSTICE

Gaston Bachelard, a French philosopher, said, "A word is a bud attempting to become a twig. How can one not dream while writing? It is the pen which dreams. The blank page gives the right to dream." This poetic insight captures the potential of communication in shaping our world.

To harness this power, we must not only understand communication but also use it as a force for good. By recognizing the biases embedded in our language, working to improve our skills, and employing those skills in the pursuit of equality, we turn the act of communication into a profound tool for social change.

VOICE AND TONE: VESSELS OF EFFECTIVE COMMUNICATION

Communication's impact is regularly influenced by voice and tone. Just as Gaston Bachelard eloquently likened words to budding twigs, your voice and tone are the vessels through which your words take root and flourish.

VOICE

Think of your voice as the unique heartbeat of your communication. It's the personality that shines through your words, shaping how your audience perceives your message. Just as individuals have distinct voices in conversations, your writing should carry a distinctive voice that sets you apart. Whether it's authoritative, empathetic, or conversational, your voice should resonate authentically with your intended audience.

It is understandable to ask, "Just what do you mean by voice?" In the passage that follows, read as the writer paints a vivid picture of a cityscape.

> In the heart of the bustling city, where the neon lights paint the sky with a vibrant sympathy of colors, I found myself standing on the precipices of possibility. The streets, lie veins coursing with the energy of a million dreams, whispered secrets in the hushed language of midnight. The cacophony of honking horns and distant laughter was the backdrop to my urban odyssey, a journey into the soul of a metropolis that never slept.

How would you characterize the voice of this passage?

Evocative and descriptive are two words that come to mind. The language is poetic and emotional, capturing the essence of the bustling city at night. It conveys a sense of wonder, curiosity, and even a touch of romance, as if the narrator is inviting the reader to share in the awe and fascination.

In the pursuit of social justice, the voice of your writing is paramount importance. A compassionate and empathetic tone can inspire empathy and solidarity, while an assertive tone can convey a call to action. By mastering the art of voice, you can navigate sensitive topics, foster understanding, and catalyze change effectively. Read this second sample passage; try to characterize the writer's voice:

> A silent crisis in looming in our world. Climate change, an existential threat to our planet and all its inhabitants, requires not just scientific scrutiny but a deep understanding of the human impact it bears. It is a global challenge that reaches across borders, affecting communities, ecosystems, and future generations with unwavering persistence. Witnessing the consequences of a warming world, penetrates our hearts to act. The responses arises from acknowledging the vulnerable communities on the front lines, facing the brunt of extreme weather events, rising seas, and disrupted livelihoods.

Throughout this passage, the author uses phrases that are marked by emotional and that focus on understanding and caring for the people and ecosystems affected by climate change.

For example, the phrase "a silent crisis" suggests and understanding of the seriousness and the urgency of the situation. It conveys a sense of concern for the impending crisis and those who will be impacted by it. Likewise, the phrase "requires not just scientific scrutiny but a deep understanding of human impact it bears" emphasizes the need for empathy in addition to scientific analysis.

Take some time to identify other phrases in this passage that reflect the author's voice, which we can easily describe as empathetic and compassionate.

TONE

Voice and tone are allies. While voice refers to the write's style and personality the words convey, tone, on the other hand, is the attitude, disposition, or mood conveyed by the writer toward the subject. A tone can be described as serious, emotional, empathetic, or even playful. Even when writing about serious issues, some authors choose a more playful tone.

> Ladies and gentlemen, step right up to greatest show on Earth—the Voting Circus! It's a whirlwind extravaganza where every citizen gets to be the star of the political big top and the ringmaster. Well, that's democracy itself, flying high for justice and fairness.

The author playfully uses metaphorical language to compare the voting process to a circus.

These two concepts are easy to confuse. However, there are some ways to make distinctions.

Voice	Tone
Voice is relatively consistent throughout a composition.	Tone can vary within a composition.
Voice is an intrinsic quality of the author's writing. Readers can often recognize an author's voice across different works.	Tone is context-dependent and can change based on the purpose of the writing. A writer may use a formal and respectful tone for one composition but a more casual and friendly tone for a different one.
Voice is a long-term characteristic. It represents the writer's character, which generally doesn't change.	Tone is a short-term situational quality. It represents the writer's mood, which varies for most of us.

Voice and tone play crucial roles in conveying the author's message and connecting with the reader, but they serve distinct purposes and can change based on the context and the intent of the writing.

COMMUNICATION ASSIGNMENT:

Prepare a 3–5 minute oral presentation on a social justice issue. Be sure to consider the voice and tone you use; both the voice and tone should be appropriate for your target audience. Whether teaching middle school students about gender inequities or presenting an argument on healthcare limitations to political leaders, the goal is to communicate your idea effectively, demonstrating the very principles laid out in this text. By doing so, you'll be taking a step towards a more just and compassionate society.

CHAPTER 4

WRITING FOR YOUR AUDIENCE

In the previous chapter, there were several references to a writer's audience. This chapter emphasizes the role writes have in using writing techniques to engage readers into the message you craft. Audience-centered writing considers the audience, and effective writers craft their compositions with the reader (i.e., audience) in mind.

UNDERSTANDING YOUR AUDIENCE

Before you put pen to paper or fingers on the keyboard, take a moment to understand your audience. Are you writing to an audience that is well-versed in the topic, or is your audience a group of novices? Asking appropriate questions is the first step, and considering the purpose of your composition must be included in those questions. Are you writing to entertain young readers, or are you writing to persuade state politicians to act? Answering such questions helps you identify the appropriate approach and author's tools to utilize.

STYLE, TONE, AND WORD CHOICE: TOOLS OF THE TRADE

Style, tone, and word choice are three techniques in an author's tool kit. Style refers to the specific writing techniques and literary devices an author chooses. This encompasses choices in sentence structure and figurative language. Style generally remains consistent throughout a writer's body of work. Style is observable and can be analyzed. It involves looking at how an author constructs sentences, paragraphs, and chapters, as well as their use of imagery, symbolism, and other literary elements. In the previous chapter, voice was discussed. As you read these words, you may be reminded of another writer's element that sounds similar—voice. Remember, voice is the unique personality, perspective, and emotion of an author. In many cases, the voice is consistent and may not be a conscious choice Style, however, can adapt based on genre or purpose.

Tone was also discussed in the previous chapter. Your writing tone should be tailored to your audience. A conversational tone might engage teenagers, while a formal tone suits academic writing.

Have you ever had to explain a complicated concept to a child? The chances are you used simple language and child-focused perspectives to help the child understand the message you were trying to convey. However, if you were speaking to a physician, your word choice would likely Word choice should reflect the audience. Use language that your audience understands without feeling overwhelmed or patronized.

Like any skill, audience-centered writing improves with practice. Experiment with different styles, tones, and word choices in your writing. Solicit feedback from peers and instructors to fine-tune your approach.

REAL-WORLD APPLICATIONS

To see the power of audience-centered writing in action, look no further than advertising, politics, law, or social media. Advertisers know how to speak directly to their target audience. They employ language to capture their attention, and they lace that language with fun tunes or catchy jingles. Advertisers even understand timing; watch how the number of toy commercials increase prior to the Christmas season. Likewise, politicians craft speeches to resonate with voters. We have many contemporary examples of senators and even presidents using language that appeals to their supports.

Ultimately, audience-centered writing is a superpower that effective writers capitalize upon. It is a key to captivating readers, conveying a message effectively, and making a lasting impression. By understanding your audience and tailoring your style, tone, and word choice, you'll maser the art of writing that truly connects.

CHAPTER 5

GETTING ORGANIZED

> Organizing is what you do before you do something so that when you do it, it is not all mixed up.
>
> —*A.A. Milne*

The act of organizing is not just about preparing oneself for writing or academic success; it's also about building community, empowering others, and working towards a common goal. In the context of social justice, the wise adage, "He who fails to plan, plans to fail," rings true. Planning is crucial not only for individual success but for creating change within a community.

Although some may thrive without a clear plan, many endeavors, particularly in the realm of social justice organizing, require careful thought and preparation. College students, especially those engaged in social justice efforts, often realize the importance of organization only after facing challenges or setbacks.

To foster social justice, developing an effective system of operation and collaboration is essential. Here's a step-by-step guide that intertwines social justice principles with organizational skills for writing:

PARALLELS BETWEEN ORGANIZING FOR ADVOCACY AND ORGANIZING FOR WRITING

1. **Prioritize Causes and Tasks**
   Not all projects have the same deadlines or carry the same weight in importance. Identify what needs immediate attention and what can wait. Balance your academic responsibilities with social justice commitments by allocating time for both.
2. **Envision the Outcome**
   Start with the desired result in mind. What change do you want to see? Visualizing the outcome not only helps in planning but fuels the drive to make it happen.
3. **Utilize Resources**
   Colleges often provide resources to support various student initiatives, including social justice causes. From academic learning labs to social justice clubs, make use of these resources to further your goals.
4. **Plan Using a Calendar**
   Note the deadlines for assignments, events, or actions related to social justice. Scheduling helps in managing time effectively without compromising academic performance or social commitments.
5. **Dedicate Time for Study and Activism**
   Education is vital for personal growth and understanding the issues you're fighting for. Schedule regular time for study and for engaging in social justice activities.
6. **Seek Help and Collaborate**
   Asking for help is not a weakness; it's a strength. Collaborate with others, seek mentors, and embrace the community to reach your goals.
7. **Regularly Assess Progress**
   Monitor how your strategies are working. If something isn't effective, be ready to adapt. Every individual and community may require different methods, so be flexible.
8. **Reward Yourself and Celebrate Community Successes**
   Find a balance between academics, activism, and personal time. Acknowledge and celebrate successes, whether big or small, as they lead to a positive environment.

In the pursuit of social justice, organization serves as the backbone of successful advocacy and change-making. It facilitates the translation of thought into ideas and plans, and those plans into reality. Napoleon Hill wisely noted, "First comes thought; then organization of that thought, into ideas and plans; then transformation of those plans into reality. The beginning, as you will observe, is in your imagination."

SOCIAL JUSTICE ORGANIZING ASSIGNMENT:

Create a four-week plan using a spreadsheet or word processing software, integrating your academic schedule with your social justice activities. Include time for study, collaboration, actions, and reflection. Customize it to reflect your specific coursework and commitments to ensure your continued success in both your academic and advocacy pursuits.

By embracing these principles, students can create a harmonious blend of academic success and social justice activism, recognizing that they are not only working for their personal growth but are part of a broader movement to create a more just and equitable society.

CHAPTER 6

TAKING "NOTE" OF INFORMATION AROUND YOU

Everyone has a unique approach to taking notes, and finding the method that resonates with you can enhance your understanding, especially in the context of social justice learning. Below are some versatile strategies that can be employed whether you're in a lecture or conducting research on societal inequalities and injustices.

1. USING A MINI RECORDER

Mini recorders are a valuable tool, particularly for auditory learners or those engaged in small group discussions about complex social issues. With various sizes and price ranges, digital recorders enable you to capture information and later transcribe it into written notes. This approach ensures that you can actively engage in dialogues without missing crucial details.

2. EMBRACING NOTE CARDS

Note cards are compact and portable, making them an effective method for research, especially when studying authors, activists, or historical events that shaped social justice movements. Here's how to use them:

Writing for Rights, pages 17–19.
Copyright © 2025 *Patrice W. Glenn*
Published under exclusive licence by Emerald Publishing Limited
ISBNs: 978-1-83708-490-6 HB, 978-1-83708-491-3 PB,
978-1-83708-492-0 EPDF, 978-1-83708-493-7 EPUB

Write a question on one side and the answer on the other.
If an answer requires more space, use multiple cards, and number them.
Include the source's title, author, and page number for future reference.

Front of the Notecard

```
1
          When is communication "effective"?
```

Back of the Notecard

```
1
Communication is most effective when there is an
 exchange of information. The people must take
  turns listening and talking. This is often a
   difficult exchange between men and women. For
 women tend to speak more symbolically, and they
             use stories to (continued)
               The Power of Communication,
                    A. Allen, p. 25
```

3. ADOPTING THE CORNELL NOTE-TAKING SYSTEM

The Cornell Note-taking System, widely used across the U.S., is particularly effective for organizing information on any topic, including social justice. Here's how it works:

- Draw a vertical line about three inches from the left side of the page, and a horizontal line across the bottom.
- Use the right section to take notes during a lecture or reading.
- Summarize your understanding below the horizontal line, and jot down questions or key terms on the left of the vertical line.

- Afterward, quiz yourself using the key terms and questions, testing your understanding of the material.

Sample Notes using the Cornell Note-taking System are included:

Sample Notes Using Cornell Note-Taking System

What is communication?	Communication is the exchange of information between two or more people or forces.
"effective" communication	Communication is most effective when the two forces are using the same form of language and when both people have the ability to share.
Types of communication	1. Verbal 2. Written 3. Physical
I never really gave too much thought about communication and how my I impact effective communication through my own behavior. I realize that if I am talking when someone else is talking or if I am looking away, then communication may not be taking place.	

Taking effective notes can enhance the understanding and retention of complex subjects, including those related to social justice. Properly recording information enables more effective study and reflection on issues that matter.

TAKING NOTES ASSIGNMENT:

In one of your courses, utilize the Cornell Note-taking System. Record reflections and questions below the horizontal line, and key terms and concepts to the right of the vertical line. This practice can deepen your understanding of social justice concepts and promote more meaningful engagement with the subject matter.

CHAPTER 7

STUDY METHODS FOR GROWTH

> Spending sixteen hours a day on hard study might make you as wise at sixty as you thought yourself at twenty.
>
> —*Mary Wilson Little*

In the journey towards understanding and fighting for social justice, I took a long time to study about issues and learn about legislation and policy. For me, the subject was challenging, so my study methods involved working with a lot of people who had stronger social justice knowledge. These partners seemed to just "get it," and I struggled some. I also took written notes during our conversations.

Have you ever been inspired by someone who seems to grasp complex concepts with ease? Some individuals naturally retain information, while others must work diligently to acquire knowledge. Most of us fall into the latter category, with scholastic growth often requiring serious study.

For instance, when my cousin was preparing to become a paralegal for employment at a law firm focused on civil rights, she would spend hours with note cards. Her dedication was impressive. Conversely, I found the Cornell Note-taking System more effective to reflect upon my conversations with thought partners around social justice themes. In essence, the most effective study method varies from person to person.

1. **Quiz Cards (Flash Cards)**
   These are a classic method to aid memorization. Write a concept related to social justice on one side and its definition on the other. Use these cards to quiz yourself.
2. **Cornell Notes**
   Fold your paper along the vertical line, with concepts, questions, and key terms on the left and their definitions on the right. Quiz yourself on these terms and reflect on their social implications.
3. **Partner Quizzing**
   Teaming up with someone interested in similar social justice topics can be highly effective. Taking turns asking questions helps both partners deepen their understanding of complex societal issues.
4. **Written Repetition**
   Writing and orally repeating key terms related to equality, equity, and human rights can be an impactful way to internalize concepts. The act of writing adds depth to the learning process.

Whatever approach you choose, make sure to allocate regular time for study and note any questions for later clarification with your instructor or mentor. Avoid cramming; true understanding, particularly in the nuanced field of social justice, requires more than temporary memorization.

STUDY METHODS ASSIGNMENT

Go through this and the preceding chapters that deal with unfamiliar concepts and create quiz cards on key ideas you find critical or as indicated by your instructor. These cards can be a valuable tool for studying for quizzes and deepening your understanding of the principles of justice and equality.

CHAPTER 8

CRITICAL THINKING IN PURSUIT OF SOCIAL JUSTICE

> There's less critical thinking going on in this country on a Main Street level—forget about the media—than ever before. We've never needed people to think more critically than now, and they've taken a big nap.
> —*Alec Baldwin (American actor)*

In an era marked by societal inequities, misinformation, and polarized politics, the need for critical thinking has never been more urgent. Despite the increasing importance of challenging existing beliefs, many educational institutions fail to equip students with the necessary skills to think independently and critically. This may be due to time constraints, lack of expertise, or entrenched biases.

Everyone thinks, but often our thoughts are influenced by our upbringing, experience, and exposure. They might be biased, prejudiced, or distorted. For example, someone raised in a family with strong political affiliations may identify with that party without understanding or questioning its principles. These unexamined beliefs can reinforce inequalities and impede social progress.

Critical thinking, however, empowers individuals to explore, evaluate, and interpret facts independently. This higher-order thinking encourages independent judgment and fosters both critical reading and writing.

CRITICAL THINKING FOR THE BEGINNER

Critical thinking, often regarded as the art of thinking about your thinking, has a rich history dating back to the philosophical dialogues of Socrates, which was chronicled by Plato. However, like the ever-evolving flow of human thought, the definition has shifted throughout time.

For those new to critical thinking, especially in the context of social justice, it's essential to consider the distinctions between fact and opinion.

- **Fact**: Information proven with evidence. (e.g., "During the end of the 18th century, the thirteen colonies in America gained independence from Britain.")
- **Opinion**: Based on feelings, thoughts, or conjecture; unproven. (e.g., "The United States of America would have been better off if they never gained their independence from Britain.")

In our contemporary landscape, critical thinking stands as a multidimensional marvel, expertly examined by philosophers, educators, and psychologists. It's a bit like unraveling a complex puzzle, but even today's definitions for critical thinking vary based on how people think about the topic. Here are some ideas around critical thinking to consider:

- Critical thinking guides us in the pursuit of knowledge and enables us to make sound judgments.
- At the heart of intellectual exploration, critical thinking helps us navigate towards truth and make informed decisions.
- Critical thinking empowers individuals to discern the most compelling beliefs and the most prudent courses of action.
- Critical thinking is the rigorous mental gym that sharpens our ability to assess, analyze, and synthesize information, ensuring our beliefs and actions stand on the firm foundation of reason and evidence.

Consider these statements. What threads of commonality unite them? Which phrases resonate most vividly? How do these insights deepen your understanding of critical thinking?

Critical thinkers must also overcome self-doubt and fear of scrutiny. In classroom environments, some students are reluctant to share their opinions out of fear of appearing unintelligent. This insecurity can hinder not only classroom participation but also independent thought and creativity.

Becoming a critical thinker involves:

- **Exploring**: Investigate various texts and perspectives on the same topic, especially those related to social inequalities and injustices.

- **Analyzing**: Look beneath the surface, scrutinize the details, question accepted facts, and search for hidden messages.
- **Making Informed Decisions**: Utilizing the exploration and analysis to make sound decisions, even if full knowledge is lacking.

Critical thinking is an indispensable tool for anyone wishing to make a positive difference in the world. Whether one is looking to question the status quo, contribute to discussions on social justice, or make ethical decisions, strong critical thinking skills are vital.

CRITICAL THINKING WRITING ASSIGNMENT: ANALYZING PERSPECTIVES AND BUILDING ARGUMENTS:

1. **Choose a Social Justice Topic**: Select a current social, political, or ethical issue that interests you. Some examples might include income inequality, climate change, educational reform, or health care access.
2. **Research Multiple Perspectives**: Investigate various viewpoints related to your chosen topic. Include at least three diverse perspectives, such as those from different political ideologies, cultural backgrounds, or social groups.
3. **Analyze Evidence**: Critically assess the evidence supporting each perspective. Look for biases, logical fallacies, or unsupported claims. Consider how evidence is used or misused to support different arguments.
4. **Write a Summer of Each Perspective**: In separate paragraphs, summarize each perspective, including the main arguments, evidence, and any apparent biases or logical fallacies.
5. **Construct Your Argument**: Based on your analysis, develop your argument about the topic. Make sure your argument is clear, logically structured, and supported by evidence. Address counterarguments and explain why you find them unpersuasive.
6. **Reflect on Your Process:** Write a brief reflection on what you learned through this process. How did engaging with different perspectives influence your understanding of the issue? What challenges did you encounter in evaluating evidence and building your argument?
7. **Format and Citations:** Your paper should be between 1,000 and 1,500 words, typed, double-spaced, and follow a standard citation format (such as APA or MLA). Include a reference list of the sources you consulted.

CHAPTER 9

THE WRITING WE KNOW BEST

Many of us have written essays in high school or emails to inquire about a job. We have likely even included a cover letter with our resumes in hopes of being selected to interview for a job that interests us. Writing is a skill, and even with all the resources at our fingertips—literally—writing well gets us notice.

Think about it. The people selected to interview for positions often meet the qualifications, but they also—in some way—stand out from the other inquiries that flood the hiring professional's email inbox.

Throughout our academic careers, we are enrolled in English or language arts courses, and once we are admitted to university, even pre-medicine and computer science majors must meet basic education requirements that includes a coupling of English composition courses. Why, you may ask. The answer is clear; writing is important.

It is the hope of this author that the previous chapters solidified the importance of writing and writing well. If you have a harnessed your voice and want to communicate effectively with an attentive audience, you will embrace the role of writing to do so. Even if you deliver a speech, it is likely that you will first write it.

Some people do not like writing because people can disagree on what we classify as "good," "effective," or "engaging" writing. Varied grading outcomes

---

Writing for Rights, pages 27–28.
Copyright © 2025 *Patrice W. Glenn*
Published under exclusive licence by Emerald Publishing Limited
ISBNs: 978-1-83708-490-6 HB, 978-1-83708-491-3 PB,
978-1-83708-492-0 EPDF, 978-1-83708-493-7 EPUB

makes this point. Essays on high stakes tests are graded by several readers, and the grades are combined to create one holistic score. Obviously, opinions vary.

For the most part, secondary learners in middle and high school write essays. This is the writing we know, but it is not the most common content that we read.

In the pursuit of social justice, messages are often amplified through opinion pieces (e.g., op-eds, periodical pieces, blogs) that are published online. These compositions reflect the writer's opinion on the subject. There is a wealth of topics worth advocating: general inequality, salary inequity, racism, marginalization of populations, discrimination against lesbian and queer communities. The list goes on.

One topic that is often ignored but has a particular importance, at least to the present author, is the empathy deficit. Empathy is the profound ability to understand and share the feelings of another, to walk in someone else's shoes, and to recognize the human experience beyond our individual perspectives.

The sample composition that follows represents the writing that we know best—the essay format. However, the composition lends itself to an opinion piece, and in full disclosure, the composition is not an example of stellar writing, but it is an honest example of common writing.

> Empathy is important but it is missing in our society. Most people are so mean to each other for no reason. Why does it have to be this way? Being mean is not how we should be. We should treat each other with kindness. Just take notice of how mean people are on the internet these days.
>
> To be empathetic means to put yourself in someone else's shoes.. Doing this is a way for us to be better humans and understand each other more. We should all be empathetic to each other.
>
> How can we be empathetic you ask? Well, we can begin by listening more. When was the last time you listened with the purpose of trying to understand someone else? Diversity is important, and if we do not embrace our differences, then we certainly cannot be empathetic to people who are not like us. Everyone should try.
>
> It is our responsibility to be empathetic and work toward changing this world. It is our world, and if we do not do it, no one will. We must commit to making this world more empathetic, so that our children and grandchildren have a legacy they can be proud of.

Let's be honest, we have read and maybe even written passages like the sample call to action on empathy. The message and intention of the passage is profound and critical, but the delivery needs work.

THE WRITING WE KNOW BEST ASSIGNMENT:

Re-read the previous passage on empathy and write a reflection on this passage. Think about the qualities that make it ineffective, and what, if anything, is done well with the passage.

CHAPTER 10

TRANSITIONING TO COLLEGE-LEVEL WRITING

Embracing Diversity and Social Justice

> Every writing I know has trouble writing.
> —*Joseph Heller (American satirical novelist and playwright)*

The journey from high school to college-level writing is marked by growth and exploration, not only in language and form but also in understanding and engaging with the world's complexity. This includes an awareness of social justice and the diversity of human experiences.

In high school, students often rely on the writing styles they've developed earlier. While they may expand their vocabulary and begin to engage with societal issues, the art of composition isn't always emphasized. It's common for high school English teachers to assume that writing skills are already honed, leaving gaps in the students' readiness for college-level writing.

UNDERSTANDING COLLEGE-LEVEL WRITING

College-level writing is an exploration of ideas, where each student is expected to present their thoughts and engage with complex issues such as social justice. This writing goes beyond merely conveying information; it communicates ideas clearly and reflects a mature writer's voice.

Effective college writing showcases understanding and respect for scholarly discourse, often best exemplified by academic journals. Even within these journals, variations exist, reflecting the individuality and unique perceptions of each writer.

BEST PRACTICES OF COLLEGE-LEVEL WRITING

College-level writing has distinct practices to uphold its formal and scholarly nature. Here's a list of what to avoid in most academic contexts:

- **Vague Terms:** Words like "that" can be ambiguous. Instead of "This is the book that I like the best," write "I like this book best." [Eliminating your use of vague words is of utmost importance, so we will dive deeper into this topic at the end of our list.]
- **Contractions and Abbreviations**: Avoid contractions like "don't" and abbreviations like "etc."
- **Slang and Colloquialisms**: Words such as "dude," "gonna," or "chick" are inappropriate.
- **Second Person**: Using "you/your" is typically avoided.
- **Split Infinitives:** Avoid phrases like "to effectively improve."
- **Non-Words**: Words like "a lot," "infact," and "otherhand" are incorrect.
- **Mixed Constructions**: Avoid phrases like "reason is because."
- **Advice and Opinions:** Use objective, information-supported thought rather than personal beliefs or advice.
- **Generalizations and Absolute Expressions**: Phrases with "always," "never," and "everyone" can be counterproductive.
- **Conclusion Phrases:** Avoid phrases like "in conclusion" in short compositions.
- **References to Your Composition:** Phrases like "In this paper" may appear immature to some readers.

SAY "NO" TO VAGUE WORDS

> Empathy is important. We should be nice to each other and listen more. People on the internet are mean sometimes. This is so bad. We need to be kind and understand others. Empathy is good for society.

In college-level writing, the selection of words is not just about conveying information; it is also a precise art that influences the impact and clarity of your word. The proceeding passage on empathy overuses vague words like "good," "bad," and "mean." The result is a underdeveloped passage that sounds like it may have been written by an elementary student. Choosing the right words can transform a mediocre piece into a compelling one, helping you express your ideas with precision and sophistication.

Vague and overused words like "bad," "good," "very," "important," and hosts of other words can be stumbling blocks in the pursuits of effective communication and influence. These words are often placeholders for more specific and evocative vocabulary. By avoiding them and opting for more descriptive alternatives, your writing gains depth and resonance. While this list is not comprehensive, here are more vague words and some suggested alternatives:

Instead Of	Opt For
Good	Excellent, superb, commendable, satisfactory
Bad	Detrimental, unfavorable, harmful, inadequate
Nice	Pleasant, agreeable, charming, delightful
Interesting	Captivating, engaging, intriguing, fascinating
Small	Tiny, infinitesimal, minuscule, compact, diminutive
Happy	Joyful, ecstatic, content, elated
Sad	Despondent, melancholic, gloomy, mournful
Mean	Cruel, callous, malicious, despicable
Fast	Swift, rapid, expeditious, brisk
Slow	Leisurely, gradual, plodding, sluggish
Big	Gigantic, massive, colossal, enormous
Many	Numerous, abundant, countless, myriad
Few	Scares, limited, sparse, handful
Old	Ancient, vintage, antiquated, elderly
New	Modern, innovative, contemporary, novel
Very	Exceptionally, exceedingly, extraordinarily, vastly

SOCIAL JUSTICE AND WRITING

Understanding these practices can support a transition to college-level writing that embraces diversity and social justice. Writers must recognize that language is a powerful tool that shapes perceptions and can be used to foster inclusivity and fairness.

TRANSITIONING TO COLLEGE-LEVEL WRITING ASSIGNMENT:

Review the above practices and identify when they might be acceptable. For instance, in which styles or genres of writing would slang or contractions be suitable? Reflect on how writing practices can reflect our values and contribute to a more just society.

The transition from high school to college writing is more than just a shift in language and style. It's about maturing as a thinker and becoming aware of how writing can engage with broader societal themes, including social justice. Recognizing these differences is the first step towards becoming a thoughtful and responsible writer.

CHAPTER 11

ELEMENTS OF RHETORIC

Crafting Language for Social Justice

> Rhetoric is the art of ruling the minds of men.
> —*Plato (Greek philosopher)*

The art of rhetoric, as defined by Aristotle's treatise *Rhetoric*, has been revered as an essential tool for persuasion. Beyond mere formal speaking, rhetoric in the academic world encompasses an effective and persuasive use of language. It has become a vital part of composition classes, especially as we recognize the role of writing in shaping societal values and promoting social justice.

Aristotle's three pillars of rhetoric, namely ethos, pathos, and logos, continue to be pertinent not only for persuasive writing but also for articulating and advancing social justice causes.

Ethos: Character and Responsibility

Ethos, from the Greek word for character and morality, is about establishing the writer's credibility and ethical responsibility. When readers perceive the writer as knowledgeable and trustworthy, they are more inclined to engage with the message.

In the context of social justice, the writer's tone, language, and presentation of information should reflect an understanding of and commitment to equity and fairness. This includes acknowledging opposing views and addressing them responsibly. Ignoring them is a mistake, as it undermines credibility. Ethos also involves an awareness of the author's reputation and credentials, aligning them with the principles of social justice.

PATHOS: CONNECTING THROUGH EMOTION

Pathos, meaning to experience or to suffer, refers to the emotional appeal. It's about connecting with readers' emotions and making them feel what the writer feels. This emotional connection is vital in social justice discourse, as it allows readers to empathize with those who may be oppressed or marginalized.

Utilizing vivid language, emotion-provoking expressions, and sensory details, the writer can enable the reader to make a personal connection with the text. When discussing social justice issues, invoking pathos helps create a sense of shared humanity and compassion.

Logos: Reasoning and Logic

Logos, meaning word in Greek, embodies logical reasoning. Clarity and reason must guide the writer in communicating their position, supporting it with facts, examples, and evidence.

In advocating for social justice, logos ensures that the arguments are grounded in truth and reason. It is not enough to evoke emotions; there must be a logical foundation to the claims, reinforcing the ethical imperative for justice and equality.

The Interconnected Trilogy

While scholars may debate the importance of these rhetorical elements, and Aristotle himself favored logos, the collaboration of ethos, pathos, and logos yields the most potent effect. This synergy is particularly vital in social justice writing, where balance and integrity are essential.

ELEMENTS OF RHETORIC ASSIGNMENT:

Select examples of texts that effectively employ ethos, pathos, and logos to articulate social justice themes. They can be articles, editorials, book selections, essays, or poems. Identify why you feel these texts exemplify the rhetorical elements and prepare to defend your choice. Reflect on how these elements work together to craft a compelling narrative for social justice and consider how you might apply them in your writing to advocate for a fairer society.

CHAPTER 12

TYPES OF WRITING

Writing has always been a powerful means of expression, advocacy, and change. From persuasive op-eds to comprehensive research papers, writing serves as a tool to highlight social justice issues and mobilize action. Let's explore five primary types of writing through the lens of social justice.

PERSUASIVE WRITING: CHANGING MINDS AND POLICIES

Sample: An impassioned editorial arguing for prison reform

> The state of our prisons demands urgent reform. Our correctional system, one intended for rehabilitation, has morphed into a dehumanizing cycle of punishment. Inmates are often treated as expendable, forgotten by society. True justice must involve rehabilitation, not relentless retribution. It is time to invest in educational programs, mental health services, and job training within prisons. Instead of perpetuating a cycle of crime, we can provide inmates with a chance at a better life upon release. We must break free from the chains of a broken system. Prison reform is not just a policy; it is a moral imperative, essential for a society that truly values redemption, compassion, and second chances.

Persuasive writing aims to convince readers to embrace a particular point of view or take specific action. In the context of prison reform, the sample persuasive composition emphasizes the role of prisons in rehabilitation. Persuasive essays and speeches may be used to advocate for policies that promote equality, such as anti-discrimination laws or environmental protection. Through carefully crafted arguments, logic, and emotional appeals, writers can inspire readers to question existing norms and take action.

Characteristics of Persuasive Writing

Persuasive writing is also known as argumentative writing. While the type of compositions meant to persuade vary, the compositions generally share specific characteristics:

- Clear position: The writer takes a clear stance on an issue and provides a coherent argument in support of that position.
- Evidence-based: The writer uses facts, statistics, expert testimonials, and other forms of evidence to support claims.
- Address Counterarguments: The writer acknowledges opposing views, refuting them or demonstrating why their viewpoint is stronger.
- Logical Structure: The piece is organized in a way that effectively presents and builds the argument, typically starting with an introduction, followed by body paragraphs, and concluding with a summation.
- Clear and Concise Language: The writer uses precise wording to convey the argument without ambiguity.
- Ethical Persuasion: The writer avoids fallacies and manipulative tactics. The goal is to persuade based on truth and reason.
- Emotional Appeal: While logic is paramount, effective persuasive writing often also appeals to the emotions of the reader, using narratives, anecdotes, or powerful imagery.
- Rhetorical Devices: Techniques such as rhetorical questions, repetition for emphasis, and analogies can be used to enhance the persuasive effect.
- Authoritative Tone: The composition should exhibit confidence in position being argued, often showcasing expertise, or referencing credible sources to build trust with the reader.
- Audience Awareness: The author tailors the message to the intended audience, taking into account their values, beliefs, and concerns.
- Variety of Sentence Structures: The writer mixes short, punchy sentences and longer, more complex ones to keep the reader engaged and to emphasize key points.
- Strong Conclusion: A strong conclusion summarizes the main points and reiterates the central argument, often ending with a call to action or a powerful statement to resonate with the reader.

Incorporating these characteristics can make persuasive writing more compelling and effective in achieving its goal of influencing the reader's perspective or actions.

Expository Writing: Explaining Complex Issues

Sample: A clear and concise guide to understanding income inequality

> Income inequity refers to the unequal distribution of earnings among individuals or groups within our society. It is typically measured using metrics like the Gini coefficient. Several factors contribute to income inequity, including disparities in education, job opportunities, and systematic biases. High income inequality can lead to social economic issues such as reduced social mobility and increased poverty rates. Addressing income inequity involves policies like progressive taxation, accessible education, and fair labor practices. Understanding income inequity in vital for creating equitable societies that offer opportunities for all citizens to prosper, regardless of their background or circumstances.

Expository writing serves to explain, describe, or inform. It's vital in demystifying complex social justice issues like income inequality or systemic racism. By presenting facts, statistics, and logical explanations without personal bias, expository writing helps readers understand the root causes of societal problems and the need for solutions. The sample passage on income equity provide details about how these inequity is measured. It also includes information to help the reader understand how to address income inequity.

Characteristics Expository Writing

Unlike persuasive writing, which aims to convince the reader to accept a particular viewpoint, expository writing is non-biased and devoid of emotional appeal; its primary goal is to enlighten and inform. It's commonly used in academic settings, manuals, newspapers, and reports to convey information in a clear and straightforward manner. Expository compositions have their own set of characteristics:

- **Objective Tone:** The writing remains neutral, focusing on presenting facts, statistics, and evidence without the writer's personal emotions or opinions interjecting.
- **Clear and Concise:** The information in an expository composition is presented in a clear, logical, and organized manner. The composition should also avoid unnecessary jargon or overly complex language.
- **Well-researched:** As a writer, you should use facts, statistics, and other evidence from reliable sources to support the information or explanation provided.
- **Evidence-based:** Through research, the composition shares examples, data, and other evidence to support the main and supporting ideas presented.
- **Thesis Statement:** Expository writing typically includes a clear statement that conveys the main topic or ideas of the composition. Other types of writing, like persuasives, can also include thesis statements.

- **Explanatory Devices:** Definitions, classifications, comparisons and contrasts, as well as cause and effect relationships are solid devices to help elucidate a point.
- **Logical Organization:** The information is structured in a logical order, often moving from general to specific or following a recognizable pattern like cause and effect, problem and solution, or chronological order.

If you incorporate these characteristics in your expository compositions, it is far more likely that you will be successful in informing or explaining information to your reader.

Narrative Writing: Telling Stories of Injustice

Sample: A memoir of a refugee's journey to safety

> Escape meant life. Fleeing conflict, my family embarked on a perilous journey. We traversed treacherous terrain, uncertainly our only constant. Along the way, we forged bonds with fellow travelers, all seeking sanctuary. Each dawn was a triumph; each night was accompanied by a prayer for safety. In makeshift shelters, we clung to hope. Resilience was our ally. Crossing borders, we faced adversity of nature and our foes with crit. Yet, our dreams of refuge sustained us. Finally, we reached a land of compassion, green with potential that expanded toward the blue skin. The land was warm under our feet and the reception we received from strangers was laced with the same heat of acceptance. It was there, amid new beginning , that we rebuilt our lives.

Narrative writing tells a story, often employing characters, dialogue, and plot. In the social justice arena, narratives can provide personal insights into the experiences of those affected by inequality, discrimination, or oppression. In the sample memoir of a refugee, we experience some of the emotions the speaker felt; we are invited into the experience. Whether a novel about racial tension or a firsthand account of living with disabilities, narrative writing humanizes issues by engaging readers on an emotional level.

Characteristics of Narrative Writing

You can dive into the realm of narrative writing, where authors paint vivid images with their words, transporting readers to different times, places, and experiences. Unlike expository or persuasive writing, narrative compositions unfold stories, whether real or imagined, offering a glimpse into the author's world or a universe crafted from creativity. While facts and arguments have their place, narrative writing invites you on an emotional journey, making hearts race, eyes tear up, or laughter bubble forth. Narrative writing has distinct characteristics:

- **Story Arc:** Every engaging narrative has a beginning, middle, and end, often encompassing the elements of introduction, rising action, climax,

falling action, and resolution. The arc, which can be called a plot structure, often revolves around a problem or conflict.
- **Conflict:** The problem or conflict is an integral element that drives the story forward, presenting challenges or dilemmas that characters must confront or overcome.
- **Characters:** Narratives include people, animals, or objects through whom the story is told and around whom the events revolve.
- **Dialogue:** Characters speak, and the conversations between characters help to bring them to life, providing insights into their personalities and advancing the plot. Dialogue regularly appears within quotation marks.
- **Descriptive Language:** The use of vivid adjectives, adverbs, and other descriptive tools helps to paint pictures in the reader's mind.
- **Theme or Moral:** Many narratives convey a deeper message or lesson learned, adding depth and purpose to the story.
- **Point of View:** The point of view is the perspective from which the story is told, such as first person ("I went to the store"), third person ("She went to the store"), or even second person ("You went to the store").
- **Emotional Engagement:** Through a composition of the featured characteristics, a narrative seeks to evoke emotions, be it joy, sorrow, anticipation, or surprise, making the reader invested in the unfolding tale.

With narrative writing, you're not just putting words on paper; you're weaving a tapestry of experience enticing readers to step into the world you've crafted and live the story alongside your characters.

Descriptive Writing: Painting Pictures of Societal Realities

Sample: A vivid description of life in an impoverished urban neighborhood

> The streets pulse with a relentless energy. Crumbling brown and gray buildings, their facades graffiti-tagged storytellers, bear witness to generations' struggles. Vendors peddle vibrant wares from ramshackle stalls, their voices harmonizing with the symphony of honking horns and distant sirens. Children, with dreams as vast as the cityscape, find playgrounds in abandoned lots adorned with detritus. Their laughter defiantly mocks the odds. Amidst the cacophony, shadows of inequity linger, an ever-present reminder of the uphill climb. This neighborhood, a mosaic of life, paints resilience in the face of adversity.

Descriptive writing uses rich language and sensory details to create a vivid picture in the reader's mind. For this sample of a declining urban neighborhood, the writer emphasizes what is seen (e.g., brown and gray buildings, abandoned lots covered by debris) and what is heard (e.g., voices, horns, and sirens). This use of sensory language can be a powerful way to bring unseen or ignored realities to life. A descriptive essay that focuses on sights, sounds, smells, and emotions can evoke empathy and a deeper understanding of any issue.

Characteristics of Descriptive Writing

While narrative writing primarily tells a story using descriptive elements, descriptive writing focuses on creating a vivid picture of a scene, person, or objective. Instead of moving through events, descriptive writing delves deep into details, using rich sensory language to immerse the reader in a specific moment or setting. While both types can employ evocative language, narratives emphasize the progression of events and character interactions, whereas descriptive writing captures the essence of a subject in depth. Descriptive writings show and they are characterized by components that may, to some degree, resemble narratives:

- **Sensory Detail:** Descriptive writing appeals to the five senses—sight, sound, smell, taste, and touch—to conjure vivid and immersive imagery.
- **Figurative Language:** Metaphors, similes, personification, allusion, onomatopoeia, and alliteration are common forms of figurative language, which enrich the text, adding layers of meaning and depth.
- **Dominant Impression:** The writer often aims to convey a primary feeling or theme, ensuring every detail aligns with and enhances this mood or message.
- **Organized Thought:** the description often follows a logical structure, whether it's zooming from broad views to intricate details or exploring a subject step by step.
- **Contextual Setting:** Establishing a clear setting or background can orient the reader and provide a canvas on which the detailed descriptions are painted.
- **Evocative Vocabulary:** Words that evoke emotions, moods, or atmospheres enhance the reader's connection to the text.

When you dive deep into descriptive writing, you can take the simple and make it splendid. In the same way, the overlooked becomes outstanding. Emphasizing on the ability to show, you can paint with words that provides vibrant details that describes a specific subject or scene.

Research Writing: Building Knowledge and Solutions

Sample: A comprehensive doctoral dissertation on the effects of educational disparities in different communities

> This research examines the impact of academic achievement, economic mobility, and social integration. Furthermore, it explores the role of policy interventions in mitigating these effects. By delving into these complexities, this dissertation contributes to a deeper understanding of the dynamics at play and underscores the urgency of addressing educational disparities to build more equitable societies. This research seeks to answer two research questions:
> RQ1- "What are the multifaceted effects of educational disparities in diverse communities?"

RQ2- "How do policy interventions influence these effects, ultimately contributing to our understanding of strategies for fostering educational equity?"

Research writing contributes to social justice by providing evidence-based insights into societal problems. Rigorous, methodical, and often lengthy, research papers analyze data, review literature, and propose solutions. A research paper on educational disparities might explore the links between school funding, community resources, and student outcomes, offering data-driven recommendations for more equitable education.

Characteristics of Research Writing

Research writing is like treasure hunting. It involves a systematic exploration of facts, data, and scholarly perspectives to construct a well-informed viewpoint or argument on a specific topic. There are often blurred lines between explanatory writing and research writing. While both aim to inform, explanatory writing primarily breaks down complex topics to enhance the reader's understanding, often using existing knowledge or general observations. In contrast, research writing can go deeper, seeking new insights or reinforcing claims through detailed analysis of sourced data. In other words, explanatory writing clarifies, while research writing investigates and verifies. In this way, research writing can be subcategorized as a form of explanatory writing. To further complicate this topic, people can also use the word "research" to refer to the process of identifying a problem, constructing a method to examine the problem, collecting data, and sharing the data. Research has the potential to add the breadth of existing information on a subject.

When crafting a research composition, there are key features to keep in mind:

- **Evidence-based:** Every claim or assertion in research writing is backed by evidence, typically from scholarly sources.
- **Objective:** Research writing is unbiased and avoids personal opinions, focusing on facts, data, and the interpretations of those facts within the academic community.
- **Citations and References:** Research writing meticulously credits original sources through citations, and a list of references or bibliography is included at the end.
- **Formal Tone and Language:** The writing style is formal, employing technical or specialized vocabulary pertinent to the subject.
- **Critical Review:** A research paper often includes a literature review section, which is a critical analysis of existing research relevant to the topic.
- **Original Contribution:** Good research writing often contributes new knowledge, insights, or a unique perspective to the existing body of literature on the topic.
- **Methodology:** A detailed section of how the research was conducted, including methods of data collection and analysis, is provided.

- **Critical Review:** A research paper often includes a literature review section, which is a critical analysis of existing research relevant to the topic.

The goal of research writing is to contribute to the collective understanding of a topic in a methodical and objective manner.

The different types of writing each offer unique avenues for exploring and promoting social justice. Whether persuading, explaining, storytelling, describing, or researching, writers can leverage these tools to shed light on inequality, foster empathy, provoke thought, and inspire change. From the emotionally resonant narratives to the irrefutable logic of research, writing in its varied forms stands as beacon for social justice. By understanding and harnessing these tools, we can all use writing to contribute to a more just and compassion society.

SOCIAL JUSTICE THROUGH FIVE LENSES ASSIGNMENT:

Objective: Utilize different styles of writing to explore, analyze, and advocate for a specific social justice issue of your choice (e.g., racial equality, gender equity, environmental justice, LGBTQ+ rights, disability rights).

Instructions:

1. **Persuasive Writing: Op-Ed**
   Writing an opinion-editorial persuading readers to take a specific action or adopt a particular stance on your chosen issue.
   Include a clear topic sentence, supporting evidence, references to relevant counterarguments, and a closing that reiterates your main points.
2. **Expository Writing: Informative Guide**
   Create a 200-word guide explaining the historical background, key concepts, and current state of your chosen topic.
   Use a graph, chart, or diagram to clarify complex ideas.
3. **Narrative Writing: Personal Story or Fictional Account**
   Craft a short story that brings the issue to life through personal or fictional experiences.
   Use character development, dialogue, and plot to engage the reader emotionally.
4. **Descriptive Writing: Vivid Snapshot**
   Write a 200-word descriptive piece that paints a vivid picture of a specific scene or moment related to your issue.
   Focus on sensory details, emotions, and atmosphere to immerse the reader.
5. **Research Writing: Mini Research Paper**
   Review existing literature on your topic. Then, collect opinions about your issue through a digital survey. You can collect opinions from people you know; this is a convenience approach. Analyze the information you

collect and write a paper to share the literature you reviewed, the outcomes of the survey (the data), and to propose solutions.

General Guidelines:

- Ensure coherence in style and content across the different sections.
- Cite all sources and include a bibliography in an appropriate format (APA, MLA, etc.).
- Be mindful of grammar, punctuation, and formatting.

Submission:

Compile all five sections into a single document, clearly labeled. Submit both a hard copy and digital copy by the deadline.

Assessment:

You will be assessed on clarity, creativity, engagement with social justice themes, adherence to different writing styles, and proper citation.

OPTIONAL EXTENSION ACTIVITY:

Form groups and share your works with each other. Discuss the different perspectives, approaches, and the effectiveness of each writing style in conveying the social justice issue. Prepare a group presentation summarizing your analysis and reflections.

This assignment is an opportunity to explore a social justice theme from multiple angles and develop your skills in different types of writing. By engaging with the issue in various ways, you will gain a deeper understanding and enhance your ability to communicate effectively. Happy writing!

CHAPTER 13

THE JOURNEY OF ADVOCACY THROUGH WRITING

The only way to write about people is to love them.
—James Baldwin [American Writer and Social Critic]

It's easy to look at a powerful article on gender equality, an enlightening essay on racial justice, or an engaging narrative on environmental conservation and think that writing is an effortless task for experienced authors. Yet, every writer knows that the polished final product is the result of countless hours of hard work, self-doubt, and perseverance.

When new writers embark on a journey to address social justice issues, they may feel alone in their struggles. They may grow frustrated or resentful when the words don't flow, hindering their ability to convey the importance of their cause. However, writing is rarely quick or easy. It's a process—one that varies for each writer, shaped by their unique perspectives, goals, and experiences.

A Writing Process for Social Justice

As you grow as a writer, the process you take to move from ideas to a formal written document may likely change. Some experienced writers are creatures of habit, and once they identify a process, they do not deviate from it. However, new writers may need help to get started. Thus, a general writing process is provided:

1. **Prewriting: Exploring the Cause**
   Prewriting activities help writers generate and connect ideas. Any action that you perform, including reading, can be considered a prewriting strategy. By reading and conducting research, for example, writers can gather perspectives from experts on issues such as poverty reduction or LGBTQ+ rights. Brainstorming can further clarify the message.
2. **Outlining: Structuring the Message**
   Organizing ideas ensures that the argument for justice is coherent and compelling. Whether through a formal outline or a more fluid structure, this step sets the stage for a strong composition.
3. **Drafting: Crafting the First Voice**
   The draft is where passion and purpose begin to take shape. This stage brings the outline to life, weaving together arguments, evidence, and emotions to reach the hearts and minds of readers.
4. **Break: Reflecting on the Cause**
   Taking a pause can provide much-needed objectivity. A break—whether for a few hours or days—allows the writer to re-approach the piece with fresh eyes, ensuring alignment with the purpose of the composition, the audience, and the theme.
5. **Revising: Refining the Vision**
   Revision goes beyond checking for coherence and clarity. It's about fine-tuning the message to resonate deeply with the audience. Seeking peer feedback can provide additional insights, making the call for justice more persuasive.
6. **Proofreading: Perfecting the Presentation**
   Careful examination for errors in spelling, punctuation, and grammar gives the composition its final polish, reflecting the writer's respect for the reader and the cause they are championing.
7. **Publishing: Sharing the Vision**
   The last step, creating the final draft, is more than a mere formality. It's the realization of the writer's commitment to promoting social justice, making their voice heard in the wider community.

The writing process is not a linear path but a cyclical and flexible journey, often revisited several times before arriving at the final product. Just as social justice requires empathy, persistence, and adaptability, so does the process of writing about it.

THE WRITING PROCESS ASSIGNMENT: YOUR VOICE FOR JUSTICE:

Choose a social justice issue that resonates with you. You can certainly choose the same subject from the previous chapter. Describe your writing process and the strategies you would use to overcome writer's block while advocating for this cause. Research different approaches if needed and be sure to include the bibliographical information for any source you use.

In engaging with this assignment, you will not only explore your own approach to writing but also reflect on how you can use your words to foster a fairer, more compassionate world. Your voice matters. Make it heard.

CHAPTER 14

THE CRUCIBLE OF JUSTICE

Writing to Advocate Through Facts, Emotion, Ethics, and Logic

Writing has long been a powerful tool for change, especially in the field of social justice. Through writing, activists, scholars, and everyday individuals can share information, appeal to emotions, and build credibility in their pursuit of fairness and equality. This chapter explores how writing plays a crucial role in advocating for various social justice rights, employing logos, pathos, and ethos in the cause.

Racial Equality

The fight for racial equality continues to be a critical issue across the globe. Writing plays an essential role here by presenting concrete statistical evidence (logos) to illuminate racial disparities in various sectors such as education and employment. Personal narratives (pathos) provide firsthand accounts of racial discrimination, fostering empathy and awareness. Invoking civil rights leaders (ethos) adds credibility to the cause, showing that the fight for racial equality is not a transient issue but a deeply entrenched battle.

Gender Parity

Gender parity demands equality among all genders, and writing has been a significant force in propelling this movement forward. Through researched data, writing uncovers the factual disparities (logos) that women and other genders face in leadership roles, wages, and more. By sharing personal testimonies (pathos), readers can emotionally connect with the struggles and triumphs of those fighting gender discrimination. Citing feminist scholars (ethos) lends the necessary credibility to these claims, promoting gender equality as a valid and vital concern.

Disability Rights

In advocating for disability rights, writing serves to highlight both the legal rights and statistical facts (logos) regarding disabilities. Personal stories (pathos) bring humanity and individuality to the statistical data, urging empathy and understanding from readers. Referencing the work of disability rights organizations (ethos) adds weight to the argument, emphasizing that disability rights are human rights.

Environmental Stewardship

Writing for environmental stewardship requires a balanced approach of scientific data (logos), vivid descriptions of nature's beauty and degradation (pathos), and citations of respected environmental scientists (ethos). By blending these elements, writing can inspire, inform, and call readers to action, underscoring the urgency of responsible environmental management.

LGBTQ+ Discrimination

Finally, in the fight against LGBTQ+ discrimination, writing provides a voice for an often marginalized community. Statistical evidence (logos) reveals the breadth and depth of discrimination, while personal accounts (pathos) allow readers to empathize with the lived experiences of LGBTQ+ individuals. The credibility of LGBTQ+ activists and organizations (ethos) lends authority to these narratives.

The crucible of justice is an ongoing process, and writing remains one of its most potent tools. By adeptly employing logos, pathos, and ethos in advocating for racial equality, gender parity, disability rights, environmental stewardship, and LGBTQ+ discrimination, writers can engage, educate, and inspire readers. In doing so, they contribute to a broader cultural shift towards a more just, compassionate, and inclusive society.

ADVOCACY ASSIGNMENT:
ADVOCATING FOR JUSTICE-A RHETORICAL ANALYSIS:

1. **Research and Analysis:** Choose five articles or essays, each focusing on one of the following topics: racial equality, gender parity, disability rights, environmental stewardship, and LGBTQ+ discrimination. The chosen pieces should ideally argue for social justice in their respective areas. Analyze how each author uses ethos, pathos, and logos to make their arguments compelling. Write a 500-word analysis for each piece, clearly identifying the use of ethos, pathos, and logos and explaining how it contributes to the effectiveness of the piece.
2. **Reflect:** Based on your analysis, reflect on the strategies that you found to be the most effective. Discuss why these particular uses of ethos, pathos, and logos resonated with you and how they enhanced the authors' arguments.
3. **Create:** Write your own 1000-word persuasive essay on a social justice issue that you are passionate about. The issue can be one of the five you analyzed or a different one. Incorporate ethos, pathos, and logos in your essay, drawing on the strategies that you found most effective in your analyses. Aim to write a clear, engaging, and convincing argument for your chosen issue.
4. **Peer Review:** Exchange essays with a classmate. Write a 300-word review of your classmate's essay, identifying their use of ethos, pathos, and logos and providing constructive feedback.

Remember, the primary goal of this assignment is to enhance your understanding of how effective rhetoric can contribute to advocacy around social justice issues.

CHAPTER 15

THE POWER OF PREWRITING

There's no such thing as an easy write; it's just that some are harder than others.
—*Tom Stoppard (Prolific British playwright)*

Writing, particularly in the realm of social justice, necessitates much more than the physical act of scribing words on paper. It is, at its core, a profound exercise in mindful engagement with information and empathy. It involves conversing, brainstorming, reading, and research—elements that are critical to developing thoughtful insights and innovative solutions for complex social issues.

Engaging in Conversations and Co-creation

Conversations play a pivotal role in the ideation process. As such, instructors frequently encourage group discussions to foster a collaborative learning environment. Engaging with different perspectives—from classmates to family members, from seasoned professionals to academic scholars—not only stimulates ideas but also cultivates a broader understanding of social justice issues. Through these interactions, we recognize the diversity of lived experiences and challenges that exist within our communities, helping us to better articulate our own thoughts and write with depth and sensitivity.

Brainstorming: Cultivating a Torrent of Thoughts

Brainstorming is another quintessential strategy in the prewriting phase. It encompasses an array of techniques, from freewriting to listing ideas and creating diagrams, all intended to harness the writer's cognitive prowess for potential application in their composition.

In the sphere of social justice, freewriting serves as an exploration vessel, allowing writers to freely navigate their thoughts and feelings regarding sensitive issues. The rule of freewriting is simple: Write incessantly for a specified duration, disregarding any potential errors. This method, though potentially intimidating initially, can with practice, reveal profound insights into societal injustices and potential remedies.

Creating lists and outlines of ideas can also contribute to a comprehensive understanding of a social justice issue. The fluidity of this method allows writers to elaborate on, reorganize, or even discard ideas as their understanding evolves. Mapping ideas using diagrams or graphic organizers can further enhance the structuring of information, especially for visual learners. It aids in the analysis of complex social constructs and their interconnectedness. A freewrite on gender parity is provided:

Three-Minute Freewrite: Gender Parity

Gender parity, such a broad term yet so full of nuances. It's like a giant, intricate tapestry; each thread a story of struggle and progress. It's the fight for equal pay for equal work, it's the pursuit of representation in politics, in boardrooms, in science, in art. It's pushing back against stereotypes that confine and define what it means to be a woman or a man.

Why is it that in 2023, we are still discussing gender parity? I mean, haven't we progressed enough as a society to have already achieved this? And yet, the numbers and lived experiences say otherwise. There is still a noticeable gap in earnings between men and women, especially for women of color. Women still account for a minority of decision-making roles in government and corporations worldwide.

But gender parity is not just about fighting for women's rights. It's about recognizing and addressing the toxic masculinity culture that harms men as well. It's about acknowledging that men too suffer from societal expectations that demand they fit into a narrow definition of what it means to be a "man."

The narrative of gender parity is intertwined with other social justice issues, including racial equality and LGBTQ+ rights. How can we talk about gender parity without acknowledging the unique challenges faced by trans individuals or women of color?

Effective Reading: Building a Foundation

Reading serves as the underpinning for developing informed ideas and arguments. For effective reading, a reading log can be beneficial, enabling exhaustive contemplation about the material. The exercises specific reading strategies can greatly enhance comprehension and critical thinking.

Reading Strategies

1. **Leverage Your Existing Knowledge:** Use what you already know as a foundation to understand new concepts, characters, or situations in your reading. Your previous knowledge can fill in the gaps and provide a richer comprehension of the text.
2. **Embrace Visualization:** Let your mind's eye paint a picture of what you're reading. By visualizing characters, settings, and events, you can immerse yourself more deeply into the narrative.
3. **Be Curious and Inquisitive:** Never shy away from asking questions while reading. By questioning character motivations, plot developments, and potential outcomes, you can foster a deeper understanding and engagement with the text.
4. **Draw Inferences:** Reading between the lines can reveal much about a narrative. Using the information given, make educated guesses or assumptions about underlying themes, character motivations, or plot trajectories.
5. **Keep Monitoring Understanding:** Always keep a check on your comprehension. If something doesn't make sense, it's time to pause, reflect, and perhaps re-read the confusing segment. Active monitoring ensures that you grasp the full meaning of the text.
6. **Spot the Crucial Details:** Every piece of text is packed with details, but not all of them are equally important. Being able to identify and remember the key details can enhance your understanding and recall of the text.
7. **Forge Connections:** Drawing connections to your own experiences, other texts you've read, or the world at large can deepen your engagement with the text. This strategy, known as making text-to-self, text-to-text, and text-to-world connections, helps to embed the reading into your broader understanding and make it more personally relevant.

These strategies become even more pivotal when addressing social justice issues. An effective reader can discern the nuances within texts and comprehend the societal context, making more insightful connections between the written material and the world around them.

Leveraging Diagrams or Graphic Organizers for Planning

A diagram or graphic organizer, also known as a word map, often serves as a concise, one-page planning tool that assists writers in brainstorming general concepts and specific details around a particular topic. Available in various forms, these graphic organizers can be tailored to establish specific relationships among

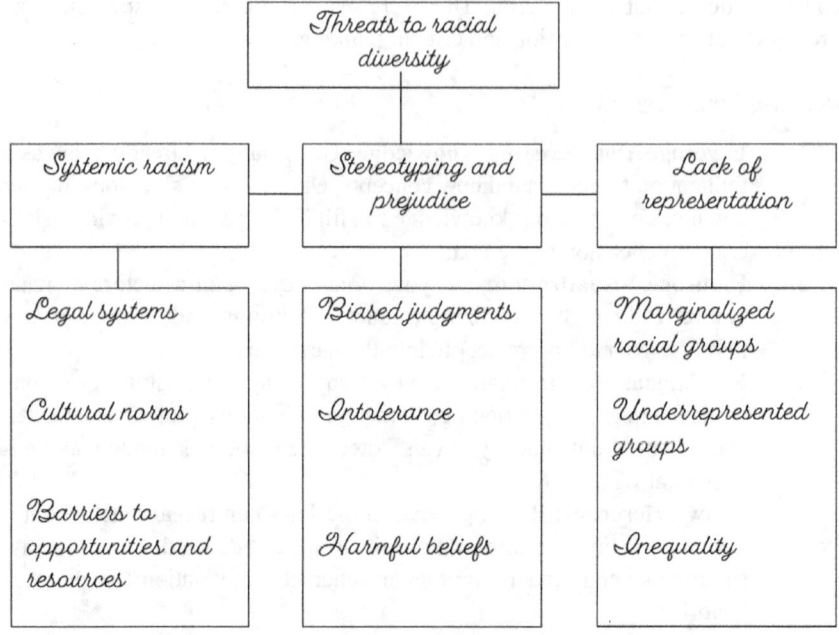

Sample Graphic Organizer for Essay: Threats to racial diversity

information or topics, while some possess a more general layout applicable to virtually any subject matter.

These visually structured tools are especially beneficial for those who learn more effectively through graphical representation. By converting abstract ideas into visual relationships, they can simplify complex ideas, making them easier to understand and remember. Hence, whether you're mapping out an essay or structuring a complex argument, such tools can be a powerful asset in your writing process.

Conducting Research: Journey Into the Unknown

Research is the cornerstone of any well-informed piece of writing, especially when it revolves around social justice. Research begins with identifying a topic of interest, formulating a relevant question, and conducting preliminary research to gauge the availability of resources. Evaluating sources for credibility is an indispensable step in ensuring the integrity of the argument being formed.

Finally, the researcher generates a list of related questions to explore and then embarks on a meticulous note-taking journey to uncover answers and discover unexpected insights.

PREWRITING ASSIGNMENT: CHOOSE A SOCIAL JUSTICE ISSUE:

For your assignment, choose a social justice topic that sparks your interest or curiosity. This could range from racial equality, gender parity, disability rights, environmental stewardship, to LGBTQ+ discrimination. You may also opt for a different issue with your instructor's approval.

Begin with a five-minute freewrite about your chosen topic. Then, conduct research, ensuring to gather information from diverse sources: a scholarly journal article, a magazine or newspaper piece, and a reputable website.

This multi-faceted approach not only enhances your understanding but also encourages critical thinking, empathy, and creativity. Remember, writing about social justice is more than conveying facts; it's about amplifying voices, advocating for change, and fostering a sense of unity and equality through the power of your words.

CHAPTER 16

HARNESSING THE POWER OF OUTLINING

Just as architects need blueprints before constructing a house, writers need outlines before crafting an essay, research document, or even an op-ed. These outlines serve as the backbone of the composition, providing a structural roadmap to guide the writer. In the early stages of writing, it is common to focus on brainstorming and idea generation. Yet, organizing these ideas into a coherent structure is equally critical. There is where outlining comes into play.

Outlining can also be compared to social organizing, a key strategy in the pursuit of social justice. Social activists, like writers, must brainstorm, develop their ideas, and then create a clear plan of action to ensure their efforts yield desired outcomes. Thus, outlining in writing mirrors the strategic planning of effective social organizing.

Creating an outline involves organizing your thoughts into a hierarchical structure, with the thesis statement or main argument placed at the top. Each supporting idea or subtopic then forms a new layer of the structure, under which you can list specific examples or evidence to substantiate these points. This structure usually adopts the following format:

Thesis: Central Argument

I. Primary Idea or Argument
    A. Supporting Idea or Detail
        i. Specific Example or Evidence
        ii. Additional Example or Evidence
    B. Another Supporting Idea or Detail
        i. Specific Example or Evidence
        ii. Additional Example or Evidence

II. Secondary Idea or Argument
    A. Supporting Idea or Detail
        i. Specific Example or Evidence
        ii. Additional Example or Evidence
    B. Another Supporting Idea or Detail
        i. Specific Example or Evidence
        ii. Additional Example or Evidence

Modern word-processing software, such as Microsoft Word, often provides outlie templates and can even automatically format your outline as you type.

Here is a sample outline focused on promoting individuality to combat societal pressures, a vital theme in the fight for social justice:

Topic: Promoting Individuality in the Face of Societal Pressures

Thesis Statement: To resist negative societal influences, young people must strive for self-actualization, embrace their individuality, and confront their self-image honestly and critically.

I. Introduction
II. Societal Influence
    A. Interpretation of Friedrich Nietzsche's Thoughts
    B. Media and Television's Impact
        i. Shaping Standards of Beauty
        ii. Fostering Feelings of Inadequacy
III. Gender-Specific Societal Expectations
    A. The Concept of Masculinity
        i. Sports
        ii. The Link Between Crime and Violence
    B. The Notion of Femininity
IV. The Importance of Individuality
    A. Celebrating Individuality
    B. The Role of Parental Involvement
V. Conclusion

Outlines can vary in detail and complexity, but their function remains essential. Just as social organizers need to map their strategies, writers need to outline their ideas to ensure a coherent, well-structured piece.

OUTLINING ASSIGNMENT

Using the topic you selected for your freewrite assignment form the previous chapter, isolate the primary ideas and the supporting ideas and evidence. Determine the most suitable organization for the ideas and create an outline.

Optional Extension Activity

Write a reflection paragraph, drawing parallels between your view of the outlining process and the practice of social organizing.

CHAPTER 17

EMPOWERING VOICES THROUGH THE DRAFT

The pages are still blank, but there is a miraculous feeling of the words being there, written in invisible ink and clamoring to become visible.
—*Vladimir Nabokov,*
Renowned Russian-American author, once articulated.
This idea speaks volumes about the power and promise
of writing as a tool for social change.

A select few are called to write because of an innate pull towards the art of storytelling or a deep-seated compulsion to express their thoughts through the written word. These are the individuals for whom words resonate so powerfully within their minds that they must give them a voice. However, such passion for writing is not universal. For many, particularly students, writing can feel like an unwelcome chore rather than an empowering tool.

This view overlooks the true value of the writing process, which is a critical vehicle that allows anyone to give form to their ideas and feelings. The process begins with pre-writing—everything that comes before pen hits paper. The draft stage is the first incarnation of your written document, otherwise known as the rough draft. Novice writers often make the error of treating their rough draft as their final piece, leading to undue pressure to perfect every word. Instead, the rough draft should serve as an open arena for free and clear expression of ideas.

Most scholarly compositions, regardless of their purpose, share a similar structure: an introduction, a body, and a conclusion. This structure is akin to a path leading the reader through the writer's argument or story.

Crafting an Engaging Introduction

An effective introduction serves three primary functions. Firstly, it captures the reader's attention, pulling them into your narrative or argument. This is the hook, the lead that compels the reader to delve further into your work. Drawing on journalistic writing principles, your lead might take the form of a provocative question, a compelling anecdote, a pertinent quote, a thought-provoking analogy, a succinct narrative, a definition of a key term, or an enlightening statistic.

Strategies for Writing a Lead

- Open an introduction with a relevant thought-provoking question
- Use an anecdote [short narrative] to make point
- Open an introduction with a relevant quote
- Relate an analogy
- Briefly relating an interesting anecdote [narrative]
- Define a key term
- Give one or more pertinent statistics

Additionally, an introduction should provide essential background information, preparing the reader for what is to follow. Never assume familiarity with your subject matter. Instead, use the introduction as an opportunity to set the stage, offering your readers a firm foundation from which to engage with your piece.

The third function of the introduction is to lay out a clear roadmap for the rest of your piece. This is typically achieved through a thesis statement—a clear and concise statement of your position or the purpose of your composition. In a broader context, writing with a clear purpose and effectively communicating it can be seen as an exercise in social justice. Just as activists strive to express their demands and goals, so too should writers articulate their purpose through their thesis statement.

Through the power of the draft, every writer has the ability to speak out on behalf of their beliefs, transforming their invisible ink into bold words that call for action and incite change. Writing is more than just an academic exercise; it's a platform to advocate for rights and social justice, and a means to inspire others to do the same.

Crafting a Thesis Statement

A well-crafted thesis statement serves as the cornerstone of any compelling composition. It is a beacon that guides your argument and incites intellectual discourse. A **thesis statement** is a one-sentence statement of the author's purpose for writing the composition or the author's position[view] on the topic of the paper. The thesis statement is the foundation of an essay or research paper. When an architect needs to build a house, he or she first must draw out a blueprint; the thesis statement is the "blueprint" for a composition. Therefore, it is imperative to write the thesis statement before drafting the composition.

Writing a compelling thesis statement is a structured process. Start by pinpointing your topic, then refining it. Following this, formulate a research question that you aim to address. Proceed by answering the question. Finally, fuse these elements into a concise, one-sentence statement.

For instance, consider the case of standardized testing. Are standardized tests accurate reflections of a student's full academic capacity and potential for success? The answer, for some, is "no". Thus, an effective thesis statement based on this information is provided in the first row (i.e., the last column) of the table. Other examples are provided as well.

Topic	Refined (i.e., narrowed) Topic	Research Question	Answer	Thesis Statement
Education	Standardized testing	Are standardized tests accurate reflections of a student's full academic capacity and potential for success?	No	Standardized tests are not an accurate reflection of a student's full academic capacity and potential for success; therefore, post-secondary institutions should use more comprehensive criteria to consider student admissions.
Gun Control	Assault weapons	Did the expiration of the assault weapons ban align with the increase in mass shootings in the US?	Yes	Since the Federal Assault Weapons Ban expired in 2004, there has been an increase in U.S. mass shootings; therefore, the government should reenforce the federal ban on assault weapons.
Technology	Digital Divide	Do all students have the same access to the Internet?	No	The digital divide reduces some students' access to the Internet because not all families can afford consistent service.

When seen through the lens of social justice, a thesis statement becomes a bold declaration of your stance on critical issues, serving as an invitation for dialogue and debate. Here are some guidelines to ensure your thesis statement is effective and impactful:

1. **The Power of Argument:** A compelling thesis statement often embodies an argument that could elicit healthy debate. If most rational adults would unanimously agree with your thesis, it may not be arguable enough. Crafting a provocative statement can be a powerful tool in creating discussions around social justice issues.
2. **Clarity is Key:** Clear language is a vital ingredient in an effective thesis statement. Avoid using jargon or ambiguous terminology. Your position should be expressed directly and unequivocally, leaving no room for inference.
3. **Purposeful Brevity:** A thesis statement should be concise—typically confined to a single sentence. Occasionally, two sentences might be necessary, but a lengthy thesis may confuse the reader.
4. **Objectivity and Evidence:** A strong thesis statement should be supported by evidence and facts, avoiding personal bias or opinionated statements. When addressing social justice themes, ground your arguments in data, research, or compelling narratives.
5. **Essay Mapping:** Utilizing a three-item essay map (also known as a three-pronged thesis) can provide structure to your composition and limit its scope. Each item then becomes the topic of one of your body paragraphs, resulting in an essay that is well-organized and narrowly focused. For example: "Due to an excessive military budget, poor farming methods, and inadequate international trade strategies, Communism was a failure in Russia."

The sequence of these items in your thesis statement should dictate the order in which you discuss them in your composition. Some instructors advocate placing the thesis statement at the end of the introduction, but professional writers often vary its placement. What's most important is the clarity and precision of your thesis statement.

Never underestimate the power of a strong introduction—it sets the stage for your entire composition. An ineffective introduction may lose your reader before you have the chance to deliver your argument. Particularly when addressing social justice themes, it is essential to seize your reader's attention and set the tone for a compelling discourse.

Your introduction and thesis statement are more than just academic exercises; they are opportunities to voice your stance on pressing issues, inspire thought, and encourage action. Through effective writing, you are not only honing your skills but also contributing to the dialogue around rights and social justice. The sample introduction paragraph considers these guidelines for an effective introduction; the thesis statement ends the paragraph and is highlighted:

Sample Introduction Paragraph

Topic: Combating Toxic Behaviors

A pungent aroma of marijuana taints the air of Columbia High School. Small cliques of students marked by their gang-associated colors, surround a newcomer about to be brutally inducted into their rank. Young women, in designer labeled outfits, boldly reject their peers whose clothes don't "cut the mustard". There scrutiny is posted on social media for all to see. These unsettling scenarios play out daily, providing a grim snapshot of teenage life across America. Such behaviors call into question the moral foundation upon which society was built. The decline in individuality can be attributed to a host of factors, including media glamorization of drugs and the impact of social media. Our nation's youth, in their struggle to belong, often mirror harmful influences. The path away from toxic behaviors and toward probity requires our youth to bravely engage in self-examination and reclaim their unique identities.

Writing a Body Paragraph

When prompted to define the term "paragraph", some students might struggle to articulate a response, while others often fall back on the oversimplified concept that "a paragraph is five sentences." For a long time, I have endeavored to challenge this restrictive notion, as it can inhibit a writer's ability to craft well-developed and fully supported compositions. In the pursuit of promoting effective communication and empowerment, it's important to understand that a paragraph's structure is not confined to a predetermined number of sentences.

Essays and research papers consist of a sequence of paragraphs, each focusing on a unique aspect of the overall argument or theme, supporting the position or purpose of the entire composition. This helps to systematically lay out and build upon different facets of the issue, creating a comprehensive and nuanced argument which can aid in facilitating dialogue and progress in matters of social justice and rights.

A typical essay structure includes the five-paragraph essay, consisting of an introductory paragraph, three body paragraphs each focusing on a separate point, and a concluding paragraph.

An effective body paragraph begins by clearly stating its main idea, often through a topic sentence. While it's common for educators to teach that the topic sentence should be the first in the paragraph, it isn't a strict requirement. It's crucial that the paragraph's main idea is supported with specific evidence, such as facts, reasons, examples, or statistics, to reinforce the topic sentence and effectively argue for the larger thesis.

Emerging writers often grapple with the question of how many supporting details should be included in a paragraph. The answer varies and largely depends on the writer's discretion and the complexity of the topic. While it's generally agreed that a paragraph can be under-supported or overloaded with details, no hard rules dictate a specific number. What's important is that each supporting detail is substantiated with specific evidence, illuminating the connection between the main idea of the paragraph and, ultimately, the core argument of the entire composition. This practice ensures that arguments for rights and social justice are well-grounded, persuasive, and contribute to a more enlightened discourse. The sample body paragraph considers the provided guidelines:

Sample Body Paragraph

The celebration of individuality and unique thought serves as the catalyst for societal progress. A uniform society, where everyone looks, thinks, and behaves identically, would not only be monotonous but also stagnate in terms of innovation and growth. It's crucial for students to recognize and honor their distinct identities, contributing to the rich tapestry of societal diversity. Parental involvement plays an indispensable role in this process. Parents and other responsible adults must encourage children to cultivate their sense of self. It's not simply about teaching, but about active guidance, mentorship, and fostering an environment that nurtures individual growth and self-discovery. However, there exists a common pitfall where adults, in their endeavor to establish rapport with the younger generation, might be overly cautious about upsetting them. This leads to a flawed dynamic where they treat young people as their equals rather than their charges. While fostering a friendly environment is important, it's vital to remember that young people require boundaries and guidance. They need constructive feedback and discipline just as much as they need support and nurturing. Therefore, striking the right balance between friendliness and authority is essential in helping them navigate their journey towards self-discovery and understanding their roles within the broader spectrum of social justice and individual rights.

Crafting a Powerful Conclusion Paragraph

The crafting of a conclusion paragraph bears a striking resemblance to the construction of an introduction paragraph. Remember, an introduction serves to seize the reader's attention, deliver necessary background details, and present the essay's stance or purpose. It sets the stage for what the essay intends to explore.

Similarly, a conclusion serves as a comprehensive wrap-up of what the essay has examined. This is achieved by launching the conclusion with a rearticulation of the thesis statement, but rephrased to avoid repetition. Subsequent to the restated thesis, the writer should succinctly revisit the key arguments made in the body of the essay, reminding the reader of the journey they have undertaken.

Crucially, a conclusion should provide a powerful, memorable finale, leaving the reader with thought-provoking insights, or a call to action, especially in a social justice context. This can be achieved through the use of rhetorical questions, poignant statistics, compelling statements, or relevant quotations that have the potential to linger in the reader's mind.

However, there are certain practices to avoid when writing a conclusion:

- Avoid cliché phrases such as "In conclusion," or "To summarize," unless the essay is exceptionally lengthy (10 or more pages).
- Refrain from using phrases such as "I have just told you…" •

Avoid using the same technique to close the conclusion that was used to open the essay, ensuring that your essay has a sense of progression and doesn't feel repetitive.

Note the technique used in the sample conclusion paragraph.

Sample Conclusion Paragraph

Every individual has a unique set of values. Most young people possess an inner voice that guides their sense of right and wrong. It's crucial for America's youth to prioritize this inner guidance over conforming to societal pressures. adults play a pivotal role in fostering empathy and promoting diversity to counteract harmful influences. As society emphasizes the importance of individuality and celebrates uniqueness, we not only empower young individuals to resist negative influences but also take steps towards eliminating widespread societal toxicity.

Crafting a compelling composition is much like weaving a tapestry. Just as individual threads come together to form a coherent, beautiful image, so too do the introduction, body paragraphs, and conclusion merge to form a seamless composition. The introduction serves as the gateway, inviting readers into the world of the writer's thoughts, setting the tone, and laying the groundwork. Body paragraphs, the heart of the composition, carry the weight of the message, presenting ideas, arguments, and evidence in a logical sequence. These paragraphs provide depth, color, and texture to composition. Finally, the conclusion acts as a thoughtful summation, tying up loose ends and leaving the reader with a lasting impression. When these elements are skillfully intertwined, the result is a composition that is organized, focused, and truly captivating. Can you see these elements in the provided sample essay?

Sample Five-Paragraph Essay

Combatting Toxicity Begins with Self-actualization

A pungent aroma of marijuana taints the air of Columbia High School. Small cliques of students marked by their gang-associated colors, surround a newcomer about to be brutally inducted into their rank. Young women, in designer labeled outfits, boldly reject their peers whose clothes don't "cut the mustard". There scrutiny is posted on social media for all to see. These unsettling scenarios play out daily, providing a grim snapshot of teenage life across America. Such behaviors call into question the moral foundation upon which society was built. The decline in individuality can be attributed to a host of factors, including media glamorization of drugs and the impact of social media. Our nation's youth, in their struggle to belong, often mirror harmful influences. The path away from toxic behaviors and toward probity requires our youth to bravely engage in self-examination and reclaim their unique identities.

Friedrich Nietzsche, the renowned German philosopher, once said, "The surest way to corrupt a youth is to instruct him to hold in higher esteem those who think alike than those who think differently." Taking this to heart, it's concerning to see societal pressures pushing young people towards a certain mold. Our media, especially television, often showcases a narrow standard of beauty: thin, fair-skinned women with long hair. Those who don't fit this mold may feel compelled to change themselves, such as losing weight or altering their hair.

Prevailing social norms also force young people into gender-specific roles. For instance, a young man passionate about the arts might be labeled as "less masculine" simply because he doesn't align with the stereotype that true men are into sports. This skewed perception extends to more troubling behaviors as well. Young men might affiliate with criminal or violent actions as a way to assert their masculinity. Those who resist such behaviors are often criticized for not being "manly" enough. This push for conformity not only suppresses individuality but also can lead to morally questionable choices.

It's vital to understand that individuality and diverse perspectives drive societal progress. A monolithic society would be uninspiring and regressive. Young individuals must recognize and cherish their unique identities. In this journey, the role of parents and mentors is paramount. They should guide, nurture, and mentor the younger generation. However, a fine balance is needed. While it's essential to be supportive and understanding, treating young people as peers, devoid of guidance and discipline, can be counterproductive. Children need both direction and nurturing to truly flourish.

Every individual has a unique set of values. Most young people possess an inner voice That guides their sense of right and wrong. It's crucial for America's youth to prioritize this inner guidance over conforming to societal pressures. Adults play a pivotal role in fostering empathy and promoting diversity to counteract harmful influences. As society emphasizes the importance of individuality and celebrates uniqueness, we not only empower young individuals to resist negative influences but also take steps towards eliminating widespread society toxicity.

The essay has a clear introduction, body, and conclusion. The essay also establishes a position, provides reasons, and evidence to support the reasons. Before the writer makes corrections to his or her essay, it is important to take a break.

DETAILS ON THE DRAFT ASSIGNMENT

Using your outline as a guide, write an essay discussing your position on the topic you have identified. Be sure to save the essay on a flash drive. You will need to print multiple copies of this essay during the revision and proofreading stages.

CHAPTER 18

BENEFITS OF A BREAK

Revision isn't merely a cursory check—it's a deliberate step towards refinement. To truly see our work through clear eyes, distancing ourselves from the draft is vital. This break allows us to return with a neutral perspective, fee from biases and with fresh impressions. Many writers have fallen into the trap of reading their intentions rather than the actual words. By stepping back, we can better align our intentions with the written message, ensuring it resonates with the ethos of social justice.

Guidance Through Rubrics

During the interlude, it's beneficial to reflect on the goals of the composition. Many educators provide rubrics—a structured guide that outlines expectations for assignments. Not only do these rubrics ensure consistent evaluation standards, but they also clarify for writers the benchmarks of success. While each rubric varies, they all serve as a roadmap, ensuring that the purpose, theme, or position of a compositions is clearly articulated and compellingly conveyed.

Once your break is over, you are ready to revise.

Writing for Rights, pages 71–75.
Copyright © 2025 *Patrice W. Glenn*
Published under exclusive licence by Emerald Publishing Limited
ISBNs: 978-1-83708-490-6 HB, 978-1-83708-491-3 PB,
978-1-83708-492-0 EPDF, 978-1-83708-493-7 EPUB

Sample Writing Rubric

Criteria	Extremely Effective	Effective	Ineffective	Extremely Ineffective
Organization	The essay opens with a clear introduction. The introduction grabs the reader's attention, provides ample background information, and includes a thought-provoking and focused thesis statement [purpose/position statement]. Each body paragraph includes a topic sentence, focuses on one idea, and includes ample secondary details [3]. The idea clearly supports the thesis statement. The conclusion paragraph opens by reiterating the thesis statement. The main ideas are reiterated, and there is a memorable ending.	The essay opens with a clear introduction. The introduction fails to grab the reader's attention. There is limited background information, but it includes a thesis statement [purpose/position statement]. Each body paragraph includes a topic sentence, focuses on one idea, and includes secondary details. The idea clearly supports the thesis statement. The conclusion paragraph opens by reiterating the thesis statement. The main supporting ideas are restated, and there is no memorable ending.	There is a clear introduction, body, and conclusion. However, the composition lacks a clear thesis statement. The reader has to infer the author's position.	There is no clear introduction, body, or conclusion.
Logic	The information is logical and insightful. There are no gaps in the information, and the ideas flow together. The thesis is supported by a combination of facts, examples, and statistics. The reader can make inferences based on the information presented.	The information is logical. There are no gaps in the information, and the ideas flow together. The thesis is supported by specific examples and facts.	There are gaps in the information that hinder the reader's readability and comprehension of the information. Some of the ideas do not flow together. The thesis is not supported. The reader is able to make limited sense of the text.	The composition is neither logical nor coherent. The reader cannot make sense of the text.

Purpose	The paper's purpose is reiterated throughout the composition. The position is supported by the author's own ideas, illustrating the author's use of critical thinking. The author also incorporates the ideas of scholars and professionals. The reader can distinguish the author's ideas from the ideas of others.	The paper's purpose is stated in the introduction. The position is supported by ideas, but the reader cannot determine if these are the author's ideas or someone else's ideas.	The reader can infer the author's purpose.	The paper has no clear purpose.
Emotion	The tone, voice, and energy reflected in the composition indicate the author's strong sense of emotion. This author seems to have knowledge of the topic and compelled by or consumed with this topic. The reader has a clear perception of the author's feelings, and the author's position affects the reader.	The tone, voice, and energy reflected in the composition illustrate some emotion. This author seems knowledgeable but not necessarily connected. The reader has a clear perception of the author's ideas, and the reader knows the author's position.	There is minimal emotion, or the tone, voice, and energy are inappropriate for the topic. This author provides information but does not seem knowledgeable. The author is not connected.	This paper lacks emotion.
Sentence Quality	The sentences are correctly constructed. There is also a variety of sentences—complex, simple, compound.	The sentences are mostly correct. There are some awkwardly constructed sentences. There is limited sentence variety.	The composition includes structural weaknesses. There is hardly any sentence variety.	The author paid little or no attention to sentence structure. There is no sentence variety.
Scholarly discourse	The composition includes quotes and paraphrases from scholarly, journals or articles, magazines, or credible web sites that support the thesis of the composition. The quotes include effective signal phrases and accurate in-text citations.	The composition includes quotes and paraphrases from scholarly, journals or articles, magazines, or credible web sites that support the thesis of the composition. The in-text citations are inaccurate or the signal phrases are not effective.	The composition attempts to use quotes or paraphrases; however, the paraphrases or quotes are awkward and do not support the thesis statement or there are minimal quotes or paraphrases.	There is no attempt to include quotes or paraphrases, illustrating a lack of collaboration between the writer and scholars/professionals.

Criteria	Extremely Effective	Effective	Ineffective	Extremely Ineffective
Grammar/ Punctuation	There are no errors in punctuation or grammar or only one minor error in grammar or punctuation.	There are 2–4 different errors in grammar or punctuation.	There are 5–7 different errors in grammar or punctuation.	There are 8 or more different errors in grammar or punctuation.
Spelling/ Capitalization	There are no errors or only one spelling or capitalization error.	There are two or three different spelling or capitalization errors.	There are four different spelling or capitalization errors.	There are 5 or more different spelling or capitalization errors.
Manuscript preparation	The composition is formatted according to APA guidelines.	There is one manuscript preparation error.	There are two manuscript preparation errors.	There are three or more manuscript preparation errors.

BENEFITS OF BREAKING ASSIGNMENT:

Enjoy your break; there is no assignment for this section.

CHAPTER 19

READY TO REVISE

Stepping into the world of revision, you begin with a completed draft. At its core, to revise means to breathe new life into your composition by refining it. In this phase, it's crucial to ensure that your composition stands united in purpose and flows with coherence. A composition that truly embodies unity has a distinct goal, with every element working in harmony to achieve that shared vision. Meanwhile, a coherent piece is neatly organized, logical, and easy to follow. Revision isn't about correcting simple issues; it is about making substantive improvements to a composition. Take this basic passage on discrimination:

> Discrimination is bad, and we should stop it. It's unfair when people treat others differently just because they're different. We should all be nice to each other and not discriminate. Discrimination is a problem, and we should do something about it.

Okay, let's be honest. This passage is not just basic; it is, well, "bad". The language is simplistic, vague, and emotionally detached. The writer relies on cliches and fails to convey the gravity of the issue. The paragraph lacks depth and substance, leaving readers with a superficial understanding on discrimination. Now, let's take a look at a revision of this paragraph:

Writing for Rights, pages 77–81.
Copyright © 2025 *Patrice W. Glenn*
Published under exclusive licence by Emerald Publishing Limited
ISBNs: 978-1-83708-490-6 HB, 978-1-83708-491-3 PB,
978-1-83708-492-0 EPDF, 978-1-83708-493-7 EPUB

Discrimination is an insidious blight on sour society that perpetuates inequality and erodes the very foundations of justice and fairness. This deeply rooted problem is grounded in prejudices. Discrimination affects individuals and entire communities across the globe manifesting itself in various forms: racial discrimination, gender discrimination, and discrimination based on sexual orientation or disability. The consequences are far-reaching; they include diminished opportunities, unequal access to education and employment, and a corrosive impact on mental and emotional well-being. According to a report by the United Nations, discrimination remains a pervasive issue, with marginalized groups disproportionately bearing the brunt of its effects. The call to address this issue extends beyond mere words; it beckons us to confront our own biases, advocate for change, and foster a world where all individuals are valued, regardless of their differences. Discrimination is not only a societal problem but a moral challenge that demands our collective commitment to creating a fairer and more equitable future.

This second paragraph undergoes a remarkable transformation through revision. Certainly, it is more detailed, but it also employs mature and precise language to articulate the severity of discrimination. It uses facts to substantiate claims. City a United Nations report is a nice touch and lends credibility and authority to the argument. Furthermore, the revised paragraph infuses emotion into the composition, evoking empathy, and a sense of urgency in the reader.

The key lesson here is that revision is not merely about fixing grammar or typos; it's about refining the content and structure of a piece to convey ideas effectively. It involves scrutinizing word choice, sentence structure, and overall tone to achieve clarity and impact. Revision allows writers to elevate their work from mediocrity to excellence, ensuring that their message resonates with readers on a deeper level.

Equitable and Supportive Peer Editing is a Win-Win

Revising is a deeper process of understanding and restructuring. Engaging with knowledgeable peer, a professional tutor, or an experienced editor can enhance your revision experience. Many educators encourage peer revision. Intertwining revision with social justice principles encourages students to approach texts with an awareness of equality, inclusivity, and broader social contexts.

When engaging in peer editing, it's essential to approach the task with understanding and positivity. Start with an open mind, valuing each writer's unique voice and background. While giving feedback, be constructive and specific, highlighting both strengths and areas for improvement. Always be kind and avoid letting personal biases influence your suggestions. Instead of making judgements, ask questions to truly understand the writer's intentions. By focusing on mutual respect and collaboration, peer editing becomes a clear, straightforward process that promotes growth and inclusivity for everyone involved. Peer editing is a win-win for many reasons:

- Equality in Collaboration: Peer editing fosters a comfortable environment, rooted in mutual respect and equality.
- Shared Assignment, Shared Insight: Both parties gain feedback from someone who has walked the same path.
- Reflective Comparison: Analyzing another person's work allows you to weigh the strengths and areas for improvement of your peer's composition against your own.
- Fresh Eyes Catch New Errors: Sometimes, a different perspective can spot what you might have overlooked.
- A Mutual Learning Journey: Beyond mere editing, these sessions become reciprocal learning experiences, deepened when viewed through a lens of social justice.

It's noteworthy that even the most seasoned authors lean on the expertise of editors who rely on digital tools and platforms for editing. These online platforms often come with comment features allowing editors to provide specific feedback and suggestions directly on the text. By understanding how to navigate and utilize these digital comments, authors can make their revision process more efficient and interactive. It is likely that you will use these same tools when peer editing.

Lastly, always have your assignment's guidelines and the rubric, if provided, readily available with working on your composition. Creating a revision checklist tailored to your project's specific requirements can significantly enhance the clarity, coherence, and overall quality of your work. This checklist ensures that you address every aspect of the assignment, helping you produce a comprehensive and polished piece. If you do not have a checklist, the sample provided could prove beneficial:

Sample Revising Checklist

Is the composition organized? _____

- There is a clear introduction, a strong supportive body, and a conclusion
- Transitions are used to link ideas

Is the introduction effective? _____

- The introduction includes a clear thesis statement
- The introduction should provide background information
- The introduction is engaging

Is the composition logical? _____

- The information makes sense, and it is insightful
- There are no gaps in the information

Does the composition have a clear purpose? _____

- The thesis statement is a clear, one-sentence statement that expresses the purpose or the position of the composition
- The composition remains on topic throughout

Is the purpose reiterated throughout the composition? _____

- **Is the purpose supported by credible information?** _____
- The composition engages in scholarly discourse
- The ideas of scholars and professionals are used to support the position or purpose
- Signal phrases are used
- The correct writing format is used
- Quotes and paraphrases include the appropriate in-text citation

Does the composition express a sense of passion/emotion? _____

- The voice, tone, and language indicates the author's sense of emotion
- The author seems knowledgeable about the topic
- The reader has a clear perception of the author's perception and feelings

Is the conclusion effective? _____

- The conclusion reiterates the thesis
- The conclusion summarizes the main ideas
- The conclusion provides the reader something about which to think

Parallels Between a Guiding Torch and a Composition

Consider for a moment the illuminating role of a guiding torch. Historically, torches have been symbols of hope, guidance, and vision-oriented action. They were, and still are, tools to light paths during the darkest nights, ensuring travelers don't lose their way. The torch does more than simply ward off darkness; it actively illuminates, revealing the direction to be taken, and ensuring the path forward is clear.

Now, apply this concept to writing a composition. Just as a torch has distinct parts that serve specific functions, your composition can be designed with a similar structure in mind:

- **The Base**—Foundation of your Argument: This is the crux, the starting point. It's where you lay out the fundamental premise of your essay. Just as the base of a torch provides stability, your introductory paragraphs ground your arguments, offering context and presenting your thesis statement.
- **The Core**—Hear of your Message: The body of your composition is akin to the burning core of the torch. The core of the torch connects the base and the top. It is often the largest portion of the torch. This is where the essence of your message or story lies. Each paragraph should emanate with clarity, each argument should shine with evidence, and every fact you present should be like a beacon, guiding your readers to understand and accept your perspective.

- **The Top**—Radiating your Insights: Your conclusion, similar to the flame's tip, is where your insights should radiate most brightly. This is the culmination of all your arguments, the synthesis of your thoughts, and the final guiding light you're offering to your readers. It should leave theme with a clear sense of direction, an understanding of your stance, and perhaps even inspire action or further reflection.

In essence, when crafting a composition, strive to make it purposeful and illuminating as a guiding torch. Let your words shine, guide, and inspire, ensuring that your readers not only grasp your message but also feel the warmth and clarity of your vision.

READY TO REVISE ASSIGNMENT:

Use the revising checklist and essay checklist in this chapter to review your composition and determine what unity and coherence improvements you need to make to improve your composition. Then, write a 200-word composition reflecting on the strengths of your paper and the improvements you will make.

CHAPTER 20

EMPOWERING THROUGH PRECISE PROOFREADING

Proofread carefully to see if you any words out.

—Author Unknown
(Did you catch it?)

Proofreading is more than just a meticulous review of written content. It's an art, a responsibility, that demands patience, practice, and precision. Accurate proofreading ensures that your voice, particularly when speaking or writing about vital issues like social justice, is heard clearly and authentically, without distracting mistakes diluting its power.

The goal during proofreading is precision, targeting spelling, grammar, and punctuation errors. But remember, proofreading is the final polish. Only after thorough revision, when the structure and organization of your composition are solidified, should you delve into the nitty-gritty of proofreading.

Proofing a composition should only take place after you have made organizational and structural changes through revising. To begin the proofreading process, locate an effective writing handbook. Contrary to what some may think, very few people are "all knowing" about the conventions of professional writing, and even among those with the vastest skills, disagreement will exist.

Proofreading can be daunting, so here are steps and strategies to enhance your proofreading process:

- **Equip Yourself:** Invest in a reputable writing handbook. While many believe they have a grasp on grammatical conventions, the English language is intricate and evolving. A handbook can illuminate nuances, ensuring your writing is both polished and appropriate for its intended purpose.
- **Mindful Reading:** Proofreading requires a different mindset from casual reading. Often we see what we intended to write not what's there. By reading aloud or even better, reading to someone else, you can catch errors more effectively. This strategy also helps in ensuring that the tone and message are consistent and clear, especially when discussing sensitive topics.
- **Know Your Areas for Improvement Embracing** person growth means recognizing and addressing your areas for improvement. If you routinely mix up "It's" and "its" or struggle with subject-verb agreement, be vigilant in those areas. When advocating for change and justice, clarity in communication is paramount. You want your audience to focus on your message, not mistakes.
- **Seek External Help:** Collaborating with peers or professionals can bring a fresh perspective. They'll approach your work without preconceived notions, spotting errors or ambiguities you might have overlooked. This collaboration also fosters a sense of community and shared purpose, particularly when discussing issues of social justice.
- **The Proofreading Checklist:** A structured guide like the proofreading checklist that follows can be invaluable. It ensures that you systematically address every aspect of your writing.

Effective proofreading ensures that your message—your call to awareness and action—resonates with clarity and authenticity. It's not just about perfect grammar; it's about empowering your voice of change.

Proofreading Checklist

Are all of the words spelled correctly? _____

- Use Spell Check
- Consult the list of commonly confused words
- Circle any words that may be spelled incorrectly and look them up
- Consult a peer or professional
- Double check the spelling of any proper names

Does each sentence begin with a capital letter? _____

Does each sentence end with the correct punctuation? _____

Are the commas used correctly? _____

- Commas precede coordinating conjunctions (and, but, for, or, nor, so, yet) in compound sentences
- Commas separate items in a series
- Commas separate the city and the state.
- Commas are used with introductory material
- Commas are used with nonessential modifiers

Are the semicolons used correctly? _____

- Semicolons separate compound sentences when a coordinating conjunction is NOT used
- Semicolon separate items in a series when the items include other punctuation, particularly commas

Are the apostrophes used correctly? _____

Apostrophes are used to show possession with nouns
Apostrophes are used to form plurals of lower case letters
Apostrophes are used to show missing numbers or letters ('75);
Remember, do not use contractions in college-level writing

Are the quotations marks correctly used with direct quotes? _____

Are the numbers nine and less and those at the beginning of sentences spelled out and the figures for ten and greater used? _____

Are all proper names, people, places, and things capitalized? _____

Do all subjects agree with their verbs? _____

Do all pronouns agree with their antecedents? _____

Have all run-ons, comma splices, and fragments been corrected? _____

Have all double negatives been eliminated? _____

Are there a variety of sentences? _____

Proofreading demands strong grammar skills. Knowing the conventions for standard American English is critical. While it is beneficial to seek help from a peer editor, if you do not know the rules for grammar, you will become completely dependent upon another person. Therefore, it is necessary to review common grammatical concepts.

PRECISE PROOFREADING ASSIGNMENT

Using the proofreading checklist, examine your composition and determine your errors in spelling, punctuation, and grammar. You will turn in the checklist. Then, write a three-paragraph discussion of your strengths, weaknesses, and planned improvements.

**The next
segment of this
text provides information
on common grammar concepts.
Some sections include writing
assignments relative
to the concept and
include practice
exercises.**

CHAPTER 21

PARTS OF SPEECH

In our exploration of language and its intricacies, one crucial element stands out—identification and comprehension of various parts of speech. These building blocks of language not only facilitate effective communication but also wield remarkable influence for advocates of social justice, enabling them to convey messages with resonance and ignite transformative change withing society.

Nouns

At the heart of language, nouns take center stage. Nouns name people, places, things, objects, and ideas. In the sphere of social justice, we invoke abstract nouns like "equality" or "justice" to activate a force that drives conversations and propels actions for a more equitable world.

Pronouns

Shakespeare asked us, "what's in a name?" Well, one of his characters actually posed the question. Anyway, using a person's name in conversation is common, or is it? Read this passage.

> Nia would not change give. Nia was determined to have City Councilman Dennis Johnson acknowledge the impact that City Councilman Dennis Johnson's choices

were impacting the city. Nia spoke passionately as City Councilman Dennis Johnson and City Councilman Dennis Johnson's colleagues listed to Nia's passionate plea.

What do you notice about the passage? What are your thoughts? Now, reread the passage.

> Nia would not change give. She was determined to have City Councilman Dennis Johnson acknowledge the impact that his choices were impacting the city. Nia spoke passionately as City Councilman Dennis Johnson and his colleagues listed to her passionate plea.

The second passage may read more naturally to you. The difference between the first and second versions of the passage is pronouns. Pronouns rename or replace nouns and point to the individuals, objects, concepts, or ideas. Instead of reusing Nia's name repeatedly, the use of "her" and "she" decreases the monotonous nature of the paragraph.

Adjectives

Descriptive flair comes from adjectives, which breathe life into nouns and pronouns by adding layers of meaning and emotion. In the realm of social justice advocacy, adjectives become paintbrushes discussed in previous chapters. They give color to narratives and help to specify concepts. "Inclusive," "oppressive," "equitable," and "empowering" are just a few adjectives that transform words into depictions of societal dynamics and aspirations.

Articles

The words "the," "an," and "a" are small, but their impact in the realm of writing is significant. Articles help to specify and categorize nouns. The definite article "the" can emphasize a specific cause, while the indefinite articles "an" and "a" open the door to discussing one of many. "An" is use with nouns that begin with vowels or vowel sounds like "an advocate" while "a" is used to nouns that begin with consonants or consonant sounds like "a community."

Verbs

Verbs are the driving force in language, representing actions and events. In the realm of promoting change, verbs become catalysts for action, motivating people to make a difference. Words like "advocate," "protest," "challenge," and "inspire" kickstart movements that resonate, sparking discussions and driving transformation across society.

Adverbs

Adverbs add depth to our language, molding how actions and descriptions come across. In conversations, they bring out intricacies that strike a chord. Terms like "courageously," "persistently," and "passionately," highlight the dedication of those who stand up for what's right and work tirelessly for their cause.

Conjunctions

Conjunctions serve as language bridges that unite ideas. They link words, phrases, clauses, and sentences seamlessly. In the pursuit of any goal, including positive change, conjunctions tie ideas together, creating a unified blend of interconnected notions. Statements like "and their efforts inspire change" build bridges between individual and group actions, illustrating the combined power that propels progress.

Prepositions

Prepositions provide insight into the relationships between words in terms of space and connection. As we explore various topics, including societal change, prepositions like "for," "toward," and "with" shed light on the purpose and direction of our efforts. The expression "for a most just world" captures the ultimate goal, symbolizing the collective desire for fairness and equality within society.

Interjections

Interjections, which are expressions of raw emotion, bring feelings to life. In everyday discussions, these stand-alone words emphasize sentiments. For instance, "Wow!" expresses amazement and admiration, highlighting the remarkable resilience and determination displayed by individuals facing challenges.

Let's take a closer look at the relationship among parts of speech by reviewing the provided table.

Parts of Speech Table

Part of Speech	Function
NOUN	Represents people, places, things, concepts, qualities, or ideas
	*Example: The resilient **community** organized **events** to fight for **equality**.*
PRONOUN	Renames or substitutes a noun or noun phrase
	E
	xample: The resilient community organized events to fight for equality. **They** *are impacting the city.*

Part of Speech	Function
ADJECTIVE	Describes or modifies a noun or pronoun, addition depth to our descriptions *Example: The **inclusive** event inspired a **diverse** group of participants.*
ARTICLE	A specific type of adjective that identifies a noun and specifies it application DEFINITE ARTICLE—*the* INDEFINTE ARTICLE—*a, an* *Example:* **The** *inclusive event inspired* **a** *diverse group of participants.*
VERB	Expresses action, existence, or occurrence *Example: Activists courageously **challenge** systemic oppression.*
ADVERB	Modifies verbs by explaining how actions happen; modifies an adjective, or modifies other adverbs or adjectives *Example: Activists **courageously** challenge systemic oppression.*
CONJUNCTION	Connects words, phrases, clauses, or sentences to create cohesive thoughts *Example: Activists courageously challenge systemic oppression,* **and** *their efforts inspire change.*
PREPOSITION	Highlights the relationship between words, often in terms of space *Example: Activists courageously challenge systemic oppression* **for** *a more just world.*
INTERJECTION	Expresses emotions and stands alone to convey strong sentiments *Example:* **Wow!** *Activists courageously challenge systemic oppression for a more just world.*

Exploring the study of parts of speech reveals the creativity and effectiveness of language. When utilized by those advocating for change, language transforms into a powerful tool for making a difference. Each word, whether deliberately selected or intuitively used, possesses the ability to enhance discussions, generate understanding, and spur meaningful steps. As we embark on our paths as proponents of positive change, let's recognize the influence of langue, molding stories, nurturing bonds, and contributing to a world that's open and fair.

CHAPTER 22

NOUNS

You're familiar with nouns; that's a lesson from years past. But what often escapes our attention is the pivotal role these words play in naming people, animals, places, things, and ideas. Nouns are the unsung hearos of effective communication; they frequently take center stage as the subjects of our sentences, directing actions and steering our conversations.

Shall we revisit those skills learned in years past to ensure we're still on the right path? Let's delve into these sentences, identifying the nouns that form the core of our language and understanding:

1. Insufficient evidence exists to justify the impeachment of the president.
2. Women frequently receive lower pay for performing the same tasks as their male counterparts.
3. This morning, an aura of triumph enveloped the room as the defendant was acquitted of all charges.

Let's break down and explain the nouns in each sentence:

Sentence 1: Insufficient evidence exists to justify the impeachment of the president.

Nouns	Evidence	In this context, "evidence" refers to the information or proof required to support a claim or accusation.
	Impeachment	This noun signifies a formal process of accusing a high-ranking official, such as a president, of wrongdoing, often leading to a trial and potential removal from office.
	President	The title is a title for the highest-ranking political leader in some countries or in an organization.

Sentence 2: Women frequently receive lower pay for performing the same tasks as their male counterparts.

Nouns	Woman	This noun represents the female gender.
	Pay	While "pay" can be a verb, in this sentence "pay" refers to the money received for work performed.
	Tasks	Here, "tasks" are specific activities or jobs that individuals perform.
	Counterparts	"Counterparts" implies people who hold similar positions or perform comparable roles, but in this context, it highlights the gender difference.

Sentence 3: This morning, an aura of triumph enveloped the room as the defendant was acquitted of all charges.

Nouns	Morning	This noun signifies the early part of the day.
	Aura	An "aura" is an intangible atmosphere or quality that surrounds a particular situation. Yes, it is a noun.
	Triumph	A "triumph" or victory is not something we can touch, but it is a noun.
	Room	This noun denotes a physical space in a building.
	Defendant	A "defendant" names a person accused in a legal case.
	Charges	"Charges"—a noun—represent the specific accusations or legal claims made against a defendant.

Let's try a second example. Explore the nouns that shape the discourse of immaterialism, philosophy, and the essence of the human spirit.

Berkeley developed a concept of immaterialism that is interesting, and this novice philosopher struggles with the ideology that objects exist only in and for the minds of people. This writer does, however, embrace the focus on the spirit. There is much uncertainty whether things exist only in the mind, but the spirit is definitely the most "real" part of a man.

The nouns have now been identified with bold font.

> Berkeley developed a concept of **immaterialism** that is interesting, and this novice **philosopher** struggles with the **ideology** that **objects** exist only in and for the **minds** of **people**. This **writer** does, however, embrace the **focus** on the **spirit**. There is much uncertainty whether things exist only in the **mind**, but the **spirit** is definitely the most "**real**" part of a **man**.

The above passage includes many abstract ideas, and it is often difficult for some people to identify these ideas as nouns. Many nouns, particularly abstract ideas, can also be used as other parts of speech.

Word	Noun	Verb
Love	Love is an universal emotion.	I love you.
Fear	God did not give us a spirit of fear.	Andrew feared what his mother would say if she discovered his piercing.

Word	Noun	Adjective
Spirit	I was drawn to his warm spirit.	I admire her; she has so much spirit.
Focus	My focus was interrupted by the noise.	Everyone was focused on the performer.

EXERCISE: NOUNS I

Directions: *Identify the nouns in each sentence.*

1. The only blues I know is *Varsity Blues*.
2. Would anyone like some popcorn?
3. Michael made us watch an episode of *The Sopranos* six times.
4. Elaine, would you like to read the minutes?
5. All of them do not approve of watching movies on Monday.
6. I ate my squash and my carrots.
7. Patience and loyalty are virtuous traits.
8. Do you need help with your internet connection or email account?
9. Kesha likes to shop for clothing online.
10. We are on the opposing team; we cannot speak to our challengers.
11. This Thursday, I have a dental appointment.
12. Would you like some lemonade or iced tea?
13. Many people visit theme parks during the summer.
14. The decision to speak to you was difficult, but it was necessary to improve the organization.
15. Xylitol helps to strengthen and whiten teeth.

EXERCISE: NOUNS II

Directions: Identify the nouns in this passage.

The presence of God is still one of the highest debated subjects in the world. According to Kant, there was no way to prove there was a God and an afterlife. Furthermore, he asserted, there was no way to prove God and the afterlife did not exist. Therefore, many people base their ideology on God on this ambiguity of proof. For some people, they need proof, but according to the Bible, God requires us to have faith. Faith is the belief in the things unseen and unproven. There are many simple concepts we cannot explain or prove, but we believe them. Why, then, do you feel so many people struggle with the ability to accept or reject God's presence?

CHAPTER 23

COMMON AND PROPER NOUNS

Nouns come in diverse forms, each with its own unique role and significance, and they play a vital part in our communication. We reinforced that truth during the previous chapter.

Let's consider countable nouns like "shoes" and "dogs". These nouns are tangible, allowing us to easily count them—be it the pairs of shoes in your closet or the friendly dogs that you encounter in the park.

On the other hand, we have non-countable nouns such as "oxygen" and "gravel." These nouns, like their countable counterparts, defy enumeration. They encompass vastness and intangibility, representing ideas and substances that transcend simple enumeration.

Within the realm of nouns, we encounter collective nouns—intriguing words that name groups of persons, places, animals, things, or even abstract concepts. These nouns, like "team," "flock," "committee," or "class," paint vivid pictures of collective identity, reminding us of the power of unity. In most cases, these nouns are used singularly. For example, we would not say, "The team are heading to the championship game,." Instead, we would write, "The team is heading to the championship game" because we look at team as one unit. Therefore, the verb

---

Writing for Rights, pages 95–97.
Copyright © 2025 *Patrice W. Glenn*
Published under exclusive licence by Emerald Publishing Limited
ISBNs: 978-1-83708-490-6 HB, 978-1-83708-491-3 PB,
978-1-83708-492-0 EPDF, 978-1-83708-493-7 EPUB

"is" (i.e., the state of being) is accurate; "are" is incorrect. In a coming chapter, we will review subject-verb agreement.

For now, let's continue to explore nouns. Specifically, we can put nouns into two fundamental categories—common or proper. Common nouns, like "book," refer to general concepts and do not begin with capital letters unless they start a sentence. On the other hand, proper nouns, like "I Know Why the Caged Bird Sings," which is the title of a book, specify content and always begin with capital letters. Examine the table of common nouns and their proper noun counterparts:

Common Noun	Proper Noun
book	I Know Why the Caged Bird Sings
shoe	Nike
girl	Tatiana
car	Toyota
state	Florida
city	Miami

Exercise: Common and Proper Nouns I

Directions: Identify whether the underline words are common or proper.

1. When you need help with your internet service, the Comcast help team is there for you.
2. Who took the ten-dollar bill from Mr. Johnson's desk?
3. Love is a universal emotion.
4. In 2007, Eva Longorio hosted the ALMA Awards.
5. Each of you knows better; you should not jump on the bed.
6. If you put that on the shelf, I will buy one.
7. A criminal was arrested for stealing a fleet of Nissans.
8. Mark Jones is the Chief Executive Officer of the shipping corporation.
9. *Divine Revelations of Hell* is a compelling and frightening novel.
10. Lemonade is my favorite beverage.

Exercise: Common and Proper Nouns II

Directions: Identify the nouns in this passage. Then determine whether each noun is common or proper.

Descartes was influential in the development of rationalism. Rationalism refers to a view appealing to reason as a source of knowledge or justification. According to dictionary.com (n.d.) rationalism is "the doctrine that reason alone is a source of knowledge and is independent of experience" (rationalism). This style of thought opposed empiricism. Empiricism, formulated by John Locke, emphasizes scientific thought more relative to experience. According to empiricists, we form ideas based on our experiences. Most adults are familiar with the term "tablua rasa"—blank slate. Empiricists believe that people are born as blank slates, and experiences leave marks on the slate. Empiricists refute the idea of innate ideas.

CHAPTER 24

VERBS

In the early 2000s, an advertising company used the slogan, "Verb, It's What You Do" as a part of Nike's efforts to promote physical activity and sports among young people. Just like Nike's slogan, verbs foster action. Verbs also express state of being and connect our ideas. Let's begin with action verbs.

Action Verbs

Jump, sign, shout, dance, crush—all these verbs propel action forward. Let's look at these words in action.

1. Joseph jumped at the chance to collaborate with the National Children's Advocacy Center.
2. The wheels of justice crushed discrimination.
3. Today, Angela dances in celebration of the victory.

In each of these sentences, the subject performs an action in the past or in the present:

- Joseph (subject) jumped (past tense verb),
- Wheels (subject) crushed (past tense verb), and
- Angela (subject) dances (present tense verb).

In addition, action can occur in the future. Future tense verbs let you peek into events that are yet to come. These verbs are often accompanied by phrases like "will," "going to," or "about to" as used in the examples provided:

1. Jayden is *going to march* with his peers in protest.
2. The committee *will debate* their position on civic spending.

As you can see, verbs are not just about action; they are also a window into time: past, present, or future.

> Nostalgia is like a grammar lesson: you find the present tense, but the past perfect!
>
> —*Owens Lee Pomeroy*

STATE OF BEING/LINKING VERBS

In William Shakespeare's play, "Hamlet," Prince Halmet delivers a famous soliloquy that begins with "To be or not to be". This phrase serves as a literary gateway to understand state o being verbs. IN the realm of language, "to be" ponders existence. State of being verbs echo tis existential question. They link the subject to its state or identity, asking "to n happy or not to be happy" or "to be confused or not to be confused."

State of being verbs, which are also used as linking verbs, link the subject (what the sentence is about) of the sentence with the predicate (the information about the subject).

There are eight state of being verbs:

is	am	are	was
were	be	being	been

Similar to action verbs, state of being or linking verbs also express time and number:

	Present Tense	Past Tense
Single tense	I am	I was
	You are	You were
	He/she/it is	He/she/it was
Plural tense	We are	We were
	They are	They were
Present participle (Progressive form)		**Past Participle (Perfect form)**
	He is <u>being</u>	I have <u>been</u>

Examine the sentences below:

> Frederick Douglas was called the father of the civil rights movement.
>
> Malcolm X was an advocate for the creation of Black sovereignty and a separate economy.

Both sentences reveal the leaders' conditions—"was called" and "was an advocate".

State of being verbs, including "is," "are," "was," and "were" serve a dual role when combined with other verbs. In such partnerships, they become helping verbs, aiding in the expression of actions or states of being. Here are some examples to illustrate:

> *Alexandria is going to the gospel concert this weekend.* In this sentence, "is" functions as the helping verb, supporting the main verb "going."
>
> *Joseph and Alexandria are buying a new home.* Here "are" acts as the helping verb, complementing the main verb "buying."

Now, let's address a common issue; the improper use of "be". People use "be" incorrectly. Consider these examples:

> *Ms. Brown be buying new clothes for Easter.* In this case, avoid "be" and employ the present tense: *Each year, she buys new clothes for Easter.*
>
> *She always be purchasing new outfits for young children.* In this case, avoid "be" and employ the present tense: She always purchases new outfits for young children in the community.

Irregular Verbs

Now that we've addressed the common pitfalls related to "to be," let's shift our focus to another aspect of verb usage—irregular verbs. Unlike regular verbs, which follow a straightforward pattern when converting from past, present, and future tenses, irregular verbs do not follow this patter. Converting verb tense is also called "conjugating verbs," and conjugating irregular verbs is not predictable.

For example, when you conjugate regular verbs like "jump" and "dance," the pattern involves changing the end of the word:

Base	Third Person Present	Past	Past Participle
Jump	Jumps	Jumped	Jumped
Dance	Dances	Danced	Danced

Again, irregular verbs do not follow the same patter. Let's take a closer look at the base, present, past, and past participle forms of some common irregular verbs:

Base	Third Person Present	Past	Past Participle
arise	arises	Arose	Arisen
awake	awakes	Awoke	Awoken
be	Is/are	was/were	Been
bear	bears	Bore	Born
begin	begins	Began	Begun
bite	bites	Bit	bitten/bit
blow	blows	Blew	Blown
break	breaks	Broke	Broken
breed	breeds	Bred	Bred
bring	brings	Brought	Brought
burst	bursts	Burst	Burst
buy	buys	Bought	Bought
catch	catches	Caught	Caught
choose	chooses	Chose	Chosen
cling	clings	Clung	Clung
come	comes	Came	Come
cost	costs	Cost	Cost
creep	creeps	Crept	Crept
cut	cuts	Cut	Cut
dive	dives	dived/dove	Dived
do	does	Did	Done
draw	draws	Drew	Drawn
dream	dreams	dreamed/dreamt	dream/dreamt
drink	drinks	Drank	Drank
drive	drives	Drove	Driven
dwell	dwells	Dwelt	Dwelt
eat	eats	Ate	Eaten
fall	falls	Fell	Fallen
feed	feeds	Fed	Fed
feel	feels	Felt	Felt
find	finds	Found	Found
fight	fights	Fought	Fought
flee	feels	Fled	Fled

Base	Third Person Present	Past	Past Participle
fling	flings	Flung	Flung
fly	flies	Flew	Flown
forget	forgets	Forgot	Forgotten
forgive	forgives	Forgave	Forgiven
freeze	freezes	Froze	Frozen
get	gets	Got	got/gotten
give	gives	Gave	Given
go	goes	Went	Gone
grow	grows	Grew	Grown
hang	gangs	hung	Hung
hide	hides	hid	Hidden
know	knows	Knew	Known
lay	lays	laid	Laid
lead	leads	Led	Led
lie	lies	Lay	Lain
light	lights	Lit	Lit
lose	loses	Lost	Lost
make	makes	Made	Made
pay	pays	Paid	Paid
put	puts	put	Put
read	reads	Read	Read
ride	rides	Rode	Ridden
ring	rings	Rang	Rung
run	runs	Ran	Run
see	sees	Saw	Seen
seek	seeks	Sought	Sought
sell	sells	Sold	Sold
set	sets	Set	Set
shake	shakes	Shook	Shaken
shrink	shrinks	Shrank	Shrunk

That is quite the list, but wait, we are not finished.

Base	Third Person Present	Past	Past Principle
sing	sings	Sang	Sung
sink	sinks	Sank	Sunk
sit	sits	Sat	Sat
speak	speaks	Spoken	Spoken
spend	spends	Spent	Spent
spring	springs	Sprang	Sprung
steal	steals	Stole	Stolen
sting	stings	Stung	Stung
stink	stinks	Stank	Stunk
strike	strikes	Struck	struck/stricken
strive	strives	Strove	Striven
swear	swears	Swore	Sworn
swells	swells	Swelled	Swollen
swim	swims	Swam	Swum
swing	swings	Swung	Swung
take	takes	Took	Taken
teach	teaches	Taught	Taught
tear	tears	Tore	Torn
tell	tells	Told	Told
think	thinks	Thought	Thought
throw	throws	Threw	Thrown
tread	treads	Trod	Trodden
undergo	undergoes	Underwent	Undergone
understand	understands	Understood	Understood
undertake	undertakes	Undertook	Undertaken
upset	upsets	Upset	Upset
wake	wakes	Woke	Woken
wear	wears	Wore	Worn
weave	weaves	Wove	Woven
weep	weeps	Wept	Wept
win	wins	Won	Won
wind	winds	Wound	Wound
write	writes	Wrote	Written

Verbs • 105

This list does not cover all irregular verbs. Whether regular or irregular, verbs are vital components of sentences. Knowing when to employ the correct verb tense is an essential skill for proficient use of standard American English.

Exercise: Verbs I

Directions: Identify every verb in the passage below.

Death is not a topic most people like to explore. Quite the contrary, even the toughest man becomes as passive as a lamb if asked to confront the death of someone he loves. However, death is evident. For some people, getting sick is a phobia; most people do not want to experience prolonged pain. They also do not desire to have someone else burdened with their hospice care. In light of such, the debate over a person's right to practice euthanasia has gained more and more attention over recent years. Euthanasia, also known as assisted suicide, is not a currently an American patient's right, and it should stay this way, for there are too many elements to consider when dealing with the finality of death.

Exercise: Verbs II

Directions: Identify whether the verb in each sentence s an action or a state of being (linking) verb.

1. The young man <u>tipped</u> his hat at his opponent. _____
2. The timer <u>chimed</u> to signal the time had experienced. _____
3. Frank <u>discovered</u> the fossil of a prehistoric amphibian. _____
4. She <u>arrived</u> prior to the end of the presentation. _____
5. Angelica <u>is</u> the tallest competitor in her age division. _____
6. Many politicians <u>debate</u> about health care and education. _____
7. Michael and Gary <u>are</u> graduates of Florida Agricultural and Mechanical University. _____
8. Mr. Jones's daughters <u>were</u> late to the party. _____
9. Spiderman, Ghost Rider, the Hulk, Blade, and the Fantastic Four <u>are</u> Marvel comics characters. _____
10. The loud roar of the thunder <u>silenced</u> the entire group. _____

Exercise: Verbs III

Directions: Identify the correct irregular verb tense for the base verb indicated.

1. It is time for the treasure; the teacher has carefully _____ the clues from the students. (hide)
2. Beverly _____ uncontrollable at the news of her father's death. (weep)
3. Charles and Kim _____ early Friday morning to meet their son's teacher for a conference. (rise)

4. Rose Marie _____ the dust off the rug and hung it on the laundry line. (shake)
5. Yesterday, the professional tutors _____ a workshop on writing an introduction. (give)
6. Many young children like to _____ bubbles. (blow)
7. The emblem once _____ the crest of pirates, but the emblem has been changed. (bear)
8. The football team has _____ the remainder of the pre-game meal. (eat)
9. Where have you _____? (be)
10. The children _____ the dog across the floor. (drag)

CHAPTER 25

SENTENCE BASICS

Many people do not speak in complete sentences. Therefore, they probably do not write in complete sentences. A **sentence** is the basic arrangement of words formed as an expression of thought. To become an effective communicator, it is necessary to speak and write in complete sentences. As you engage in verbal conversation, think about the words before you use them. Express yourself in complete sentences. This will help you think in complete sentences, and naturally, you will begin writing in complete sentences.

SUBJECTS AND PREDICATES

Subjects

Consequently, the first step is to clarify the word "sentence." Again, a sentence is a group of words arranged to express a complete idea. There are two building blocks of a sentence—a subject and a predicate. The subject and predicate work together. The subject is usually a noun or a group of words, including at least one noun.

To identify the subject in a sentence, you must determine the person, thing, or idea performing an action **or** the person, thing, or idea to which the sentence is referring. If you removed all nonessential words from the subject, you would be left with the simple subject. The **simple subject** is the only essential word of the subject.

Examine the sentences below.

1. The American public severely scrutinized Don Imus for his comments about the Rutger's basketball team.
    What person, thing, or idea is performing an action or being discussed in this sentence?—the American public
    The American public *is the subject of the sentence.*
    Public *is the simple subject.*
2. Ultimately, Imus lost his job.
    What person, thing, or idea is performing an action or being discussed in this sentence?—Imus
    Imus *is the subject of the sentence [simple subject].*
3. Many public figures speak freely about people of other genders, ethnicities, and classifications.
    What person, thing, or idea is performing an action or being discussed in this sentence?—Many public figures
    Public figures *is the subject of the sentence.*
    Figures *is the simple subject.*
4. The First Amendment affords Americans the freedom of speech.
    What person, thing, or idea is performing an action or being discussed in this sentence?—The First Amendment
    The First Amendment *is the subject of the sentence.*
    The First Amendment is name of one of the amendments of the Constitution. Therefore, you cannot break up these words. **The First Amendment** *is the simple subject.*
5. Poor judgment is not an excuse for a person's actions.
    What person, thing, or idea is performing an action or being discussed in this sentence?—Poor judgment
    Poor judgment *is the subject.*
    Judgment *is the simple subject.*

Predicates

A **predicate** is the word or words that discuss the subject or reveal the action of the subject. A verb, a word or word phrase expressing action or linking ideas, is usually the most essential part of the predicate—the **simple predicate**.

Examine the same sentences.

1. The American public severely scrutinized Don Imus for his comments about the Rutger's basketball team.
    What person, thing, or idea is performing an action or being discussed in this sentence?—The American public

What did the American public do? They **severely _scrutinized_ Don Imus for his comments about the Rutgers basketball team**.
  Severely _scrutinized_ Don Imus for his comments about the Rutgers basketball team *is the complete predicate.*
  Scrutinized *is the verb or simple predicate.*
2. Ultimately, Imus lost his job.
  What person, thing, or idea is performing an action or being discussed in this sentence?—Imus
  *What did Imus do? He **_lost_ his job**.*
  Lost his job *is the complete predicate.*
  Lost *is the verb [simple predicate].*
3. Many public figures speak freely about people of other genders, ethnicities, and classifications.
  What person, thing, or idea is performing an action or being discussed in this sentence?—Many public figures
  *What action do many public figures perform? They **_speak_ freely about people of other genders, ethnicities, and classifications**.*
  Speak freely about people of other genders, ethnicities, and classifications *is the complete predicate.*
  Speak *is the verb [simple predicate].*
4. The First Amendment affords Americans the freedom of speech.
  What person, thing, or idea is performing an action or being discussed in this sentence?—The First Amendment
  *What does The First Amendment do? It **_affords_ Americans the freedom of speech.***
  Affords Americans the freedom of speech *is the complete predicate.*
  Affords *is the verb [simple predicate].*
5. Poor judgment is not an excuse for a person's actions.
  What person, thing, or idea is performing an action or being discussed in this sentence?—Poor judgment
  *What does the sentence reveal about poor judgment? It **_is_ not an excuse for a person's actions.***
  _Is_ not an excuse for a person's actions *is the complete predicate.*
  _Is_ *is the verb [simple predicate].*

Compound Subjects

Some sentences contain compound subjects. A **compound subject** is a subject that includes more than one noun. Often, compound subjects are joined by the word **and**; however, this is not always the case.

Examine the sentences below:

1. Kesha and Gregory debated and compromised for two hours.
  What is the subject in this sentence?—Angela and Gregory

2. *The Color Purple* and *Possessing the Secret of Joy* are written by the same author.
    What is the subject in this sentence?—*The Color Purple* and *Possessing the Secret of Joy*
3. The director and the assistant director will come to our meeting today.
    What is the subject in this sentence?—the director and the assistant director
4. Jamal, Sean, and Maxwell were injured in last night's game.
    What is the subject in this sentence?—Jamal, Sean, and Maxwell
5. Mr. Johnson and she have decided to accept the proposal.
    What is the subject in this sentence?—Mr. Johnson and she

Compound Verbs [simple predicates]

Some sentences include compound simple predicates. A **compound predicate** consists of two or more verbs relating to the subject.

Examine the sentences below.

1. Kesha and Gregory debated and compromised ed for two hours.
    What is the complete predicate in this sentence? –**debated and compromised for two hours.**
    What is the compound simple predicate [verb]?—**debated and compromised**
2. Danny overslept and missed the interview.
    What is the complete predicate in this sentence?—**overslept and missed the interview**
    What is the compound simple predicate [verb]?—**overslept and missed**
3. I drank and ate right before getting in the swimming pool.
    What is the complete predicate?—**drank and ate right before getting in the swimming pool**
    What is the compound simple predicate [verb]?—**drank and ate**
4. The computer quickly processed and saved the information.
    What is the complete predicate?—quickly **processed and saved the information**
    What is the compound simple predicate [verb]?—**processed and saved**
5. The student examined her composition and made the necessary changes.
    What is the complete predicate?—**examined her composition and made the necessary changes**
    What is the compound simple predicate [verb]?—**examined and made**

Implied Subjects

Imperative sentences give commands. Often, these sentences begin with the verb and do not include a name or direct subject. In such cases, the subject is an implied second person—you. Examine the examples below.

1. Do not board the train without a boarding pass.—*The subject of the sentence is "you."*
2. Call me when you get home.—*Again, the subject of the sentence is "you."*
3. Clean the bottom side of the DVD with straight strokes from the DVD's center to the outer rim only.—*The subject of the sentence is "you."*

Questions

Identifying the subject and predicate of an interrogative sentence, or question, can prove difficult. Even in a question, you must identify who or what is doing something of being discussed in the sentence. Examine the examples below.

1. Does Adam have the same values as his mother? —-*Adam is the subject. Does have is the verb phrase.*
   Who won the art competition?—Who is the subject. Won is the verb.

SUBJECTS AND PREDICATES ASSIGNMENT

Print a copy of your essay. Underline the complete subject once and the complete predicate twice. Complete the regime for each sentence in your essay. Yes, the whole essay!

Exercise: Subjects and Predicates I

Directions: Underline the complete subject and circle the complete predicate.

1. Mr. Jones works every day except Sunday.
2. Bill's unexpected termination caused a delay in the production of the blueprints and increased the other employee's work load.
3. My mom likes to bake pastries and decorate layer cakes.
4. Education is pivotal for professional and social development.
5. College prepares students for professional development that will occur on the job.
6. Many people fear that which they do not understand.
7. Familiarity is a solid measure of social impact.
8. Octavia E. Butler, an African American science fiction author, wrote *Kindred* and *Dawn*.
9. The curriculum committee meets the first Friday of each month.

10. John and Bill, along with Adam and Jason, were recommended and selected for the future leaders program.

Exercise: Subjects and Predicates II

Directions: Underline the complete subject and circle the complete predicate. Write "implied subject you" if applicable.

1. During lunch, Sarah purchased a three-course meal and ate her dessert first.
2. The game looks fun but seems challenging.
3. With a little help from Jamal, Jacob constructed a tree house for his niece and nephew.
4. Jermaine's brother and sister competed in the regional tennis tournament for pairs and won.
5. The three friends, along with their husbands, found a remote cabin for their vacation.
6. Discuss the topic with other members first.
7. Anthony played defensive tackle for the University of Hawaii.
8. Shawn opened an organic market in down town Chicago.
9. Never clean the bar code area or get it wet.
10. The area has a plush foliage landscape and its close to a city park.

CHAPTER 26

MAKING SUBJECTS AND VERBS AGREE

In a sentence, a subject and verb work together; therefore, the subject and verb must agree in number. The subject of a sentence is either singular (from single, meaning "one") or plural (more than one). If the subject of the sentence is singular, the verb must also be singular. Likewise, if the subject of a sentence is plural, the verbs must be plural.

Examine the examples below:

Jermaine advocates for improved federal services for Americans 60 and over.

However, Sade and Jermaine advocate for improved federal services for Americans 60 and over.

In the first example, **Jermaine** is the subject. Jermaine, one individual, is one unit. Therefore, the subject of the first sentence is singular. The verb, **advocates**, is also singular.

At this point, you probably have a logical QUESTION:

ANSWER: Most of the time, a singular verb ends with "s".

How can I distinguish a singular verb from a plural verb?

Singular Verb	Plural Verb
Purchases	Purchase
Sings	Sing
Begins	Begin
Discovers	Discover

EXCEPTION: The first person subject "I" and the second person subject "you" are exceptions to the rule.

You would not write, I advocates for improved federal services for Americans 60 and over.

Neither would you write, You advicates for improved federal services for Americans 60 and over.

Instead, you would use the plural version of the verb:

I advocate or improved federal services for Americans 60 and over. You advocate for improved federal services for Americans 60 and over.

MAKING SUBJECTS AND VERBS AGREE

Indefinite Pronouns

When an indefinite pronoun is the subject of a sentence, the verb must agree with the pronoun in number.

SINGULAR— Certain indefinite pronouns are always singular, and to make the subject agree with the verb, the writer must use a singular verb.

SINGULAR

anybody	either	neither	one
anyone	everybody	nobody	somebody
each	everyone	no one	someone

Each of the scholarships has an essay requirement.
Everyone is required to attend the meeting.

PLURAL— Five indefinite pronouns are always plural, and to make the subject agree with the verb, the writer must use a plural verb.

PLURAL

| both | few | many | others | several |

Both of the poems were published in this month's issue of *Ebony*.
Few of the students have the correct assignment.

SINGULAR OR PLURAL— Depending upon how each is used in the sentence, five indefinite pronouns may be singular or plural. If the pronoun is singular, use a singular verb. If the pronoun is plural, use a plural verb.

SINGULAR OR PLURAL

all   any   most   none   some

Some of the students are going to the workshop.
All of the cookie has been eaten.

MAKING SUBJECTS AND VERBS AGREE ASSIGNMENT

Using the same printed copy of the essay you used for the subjects and predicates assignment, circle the subject and verb of each sentence. Make sure the subject agrees with verb. If the subject does not agree with the verb, change the sentence so they do agree. Be sure to make the corrections on the electronic version you have saved on your flash drive.

Exercise: Subject and Verb Agreement I

According to Abraham Lincoln, "most folks are as happy as they make up their minds to be;" this quote (concern, concerns) many aspects of daily life. First, many people (do, does) not recognize they (has, have) a choice. Essentially, life is about choices. A person (chooses, choose) his own professional and personal path, but he also can choose his own emotional condition. If he (want, wants) happiness, he has to choose happiness. Lincoln's statement (is, are) also applicable to how adversities (affect, affects) individuals. Many people (are, is) diverted by problems. Extreme cases of such can lead to depression or even suicide. However, a person (does, do) not have to change his emotional state because of circumstances. Ultimately, most people will experience pain and sadness, but a person (chooses, choose) to allow the hurt to overwhelm his life. Finally, different people perceive happiness differently. Many people (associate, associates) the acquisition of money and material objects with their happiness. If a person's happiness (is, are) dependent upon material possessions, he (are, is) allowing an external force to control his internal wellness.

Exercise: Subject and Verb Agreement II

A commitment to life-long learning (is, are) essential to individual development. Education (are, is) a process of self discovery—discovery of self and society. The more a person learns, the more he (begins, begin) to confront himself and the society in which he (dwell, dwells). Therefore, individuals must embrace learning for their own benefit. Learning also (provides, provide) exposure. Many people (are, is) limited in their choice for a career, for they (are, is) unaware of certain careers. However, learning (opens, open) an individual up to unlimited professional and personal possibilities. Additionally, in Proverbs 4:13 (n.d.), the Bible states, "Hold on to instruction, do not let it go; guard it well, for it is your life." This passage (reveal, reveals) the importance of learning. The quote (states, state), "for it is your life." This statement is powerful. The words reveal that learning (is, are) essential, for life itself (depend, depends) upon "instruction" and the acquisition of knowledge.

Exercise: Subject and Verb Agreement III

There (are, is) many benefits of a college education. First, a college education could lead to a better job. Certain careers (require, requires) applicants to hold a college degree. For example, to become an architect, an individual must obtain a bachelor's degree. Most employers also (pay, pays) college-degreed applicants more than non-degree applicants. A college education also (promote, promotes) self development. Individuality (is, are) an essential aspect of education. Each person must work on his strengths and weaknesses, and college (allows, allow) for such personal development. Finally, most college graduates (earn, earns) more money than high school graduates. On average, college graduates (earn, earns) 33% more than high school graduates. Over a lifetime, this could amount to a million-dollar difference.

Exercise: Subject and Verb Agreement IV

Computers are probably the most helpful inventions of all time. Computers (make, makes) tasks faster. Whether the user (are, is) sending email or using instant messenger, computers (allows, allow) people to communicate easier and cheaper than other methods of communication. For example, the cost of most cellular phone plans (is, are) based on the number of minutes spent on the phone; however, a user can instant message or email someone as much as he would like without incurring additional charges to his internet bill. Computers (are, is) useful for more than communication. A user can use a computer to store information and documents. College students (finds, find) this particularly beneficial for students (write, writes) many papers. Having the ability to compose a paper and go back to it to make changes (save, saves) time. Finally, computers (are, is) useful for entertainment. A user can use the computer to watch DVDs and play music CDs or games on CD. Using a computer, a user can also download CDs and DVDs from the Internet.

CHAPTER 27

PUNCTUATING SENTENCES

A **sentence** is an independent grammatical unit of expression. A sentence expresses a complete thought. There are three types of sentences: simple, compound, and complex.

There are different ways to format sentences.

SIMPLE SENTENCES

One independent clause.

James facilitated the study skills workshop.

An **independent clause** is a group of words that contains a subject and a verb and expresses a complete thought.

COMPOUND SENTENCES

Independent clause semicolon independent clause.

James facilitated the study skills workshop; Kesha facilitated the student success workshop.

Independent clause **comma** coordinating conjunction independent clause.
James facilitated the study skills workshop, and Kesha facilitated the student success workshop.
There are several coordinating conjunctions: and, but, for, nor, or, so, yet
Independent clause **semicolon** *independent marker* **comma** independent clause.
James facilitated the study skills workshop; however, Kesha facilitated the student success workshop.

COMPLEX SENTENCES

A **dependent clause** contains a subject and a verb, but it does not express a complete thought.

Dependent marker dependent clause **comma** independent clause.
Because James facilitated the study skills workshop, Kesha facilitated the student success workshop.
Common Dependent Makers: after, although, as, as if, because, before, if, since, then, until, when, while

Independent clause dependent maker dependent clause.
James facilitated the study skills workshop since Kesha facilitated the student success workshop.

First part of independent clause **comma** non essential clause or phrase **comma** the rest of independent clause.
James, the Student Life Coordinator, facilitated the study skills workshop.

First part of independent clause essential clause or phrase rest of the independent clause.
Many instructors who also facilitate workshops congratulated James on his presentation.

PUNCTUATING SENTENCES ASSIGNMENT

Print an additional copy of your essay. Examine each sentence of your essay for punctuation errors. Use the editing mark on page 70 to make the appropriate changes to your composition. Be sure to make the changes on the electronic version of your essay stored on your jump drive.

Exercise: Punctuating Sentences I

Directions: Read each sentence carefully, and add the appropriate punctuation to the sentences.

1. The disaster at the beach was unfortunate however no one was hurt
2. Andrew displayed his anger toward the group but he was really made at himself
3. Jason was pleased that his father came to his game but his father did not understand the game
4. Charlesetta and Rodnetta were name after their fathers Charles and Rodney
5. The precocious girl reacted in fear at the sight of the fake mummy she thought the mummy was real
6. It is wonderful to have faith Simon but do not use God as an excuse
7. Although there is only a twenty five percent chance of rain we will reschedule the barbeque until next week
8. The artist whose work is on display received a generous check from an art museum proprietor
9. A brutal murder was caught on tape the attacker is still at large
10. Do you suffer from frequent headaches or do you have a problem sleeping

Exercise: Punctuating Sentences II

Directions: Carefully read the paragraph. Add the correct punctuation where necessary.

To obtain a career after high school is a good path to choose but there are more benefits you can acquire by going to college. College brings out self development and proper etiquette skills when pursuing your career Higher learning gives you knowledge and a better understanding of life College gives an experience in associating with people and learning more than what you already know The more you are educated the more money you reap and the more successful you become Some careers requires a college education so it will benefit you immensely to rely on college before choosing a career.

CHAPTER 28

ADJECTIVES AND ADVERBS

Adjectives are words that describe or modify nouns. An **adverb** modifies or describes a verb, adjective, or another adverb. Adverbs commonly end with –ly. However, this is not always the case.

Adjective	Adverb	Example
Warm		It is warm outside.
	Warmly	He warmly smiled at her.
Bright		The new car is bright.
	Brightly	The car shines brightly.
Careless		The operator was careless.
	Carelessly	The caregiver behaved carelessly.
Bad		He is a bad little boy.
	Badly	She behaved badly.
Real		His real name is Adam.
	Really	He really sounds optimistic about conference.
Quick		The runner is quick.
	Quickly	The event was over quickly.

Some words are both adjectives and adverbs.

Adjective	Adverb	Example
Fast		She is fast.
	Fast	The musician played fast.
Early		The technician is early.
	Early	The technician arrived early.
Late		He is late.
	Late	He arrived late.

Some adverbs modify adjectives or other adverbs. Examine the examples below:

Sentence	Adverb(s)	Explanation
Amanda sings extremely well.	Extremely Well	"Well" is an adverb because it explains how Amanda sings. "Extremely" is an adverb because it modifies the adverb "well."
Victor dresses very professionally.	Very Professionally	"Professionally" is an adverb because it explains how Victor dresses. "Very" is an adverb because it modifies the adverb "professionally."
Jonathan is very angry.	Very Angry	"Angry" is an adjective it describes Jonathan. "Very" is an adverb that modifies "angry."

Good/Well

Many people confuse the adjective **good** with the adverb **well**. Examine the sentences below:

Despite the news, he is **good**.

Although she is ill, he feels **well**.

She is a **good** chef. She cooks **well**.

Articles

An **article** is an adjective used next to a noun to There are only three articles in American English—**a, an, the.**

The is the indefinite article. The indefinite article is used before singular and plural nouns that refer to a particular member of a group.

An/a are definite articles. A definite article is used before singular nouns that refer to any member of a group. Use **an** with words that begin with a vowel or vowel sound—**an hour, an apple, an alligator, an egg, an igloo, an owl, an umbrella.**

Use **a** with nouns that begin with a consonant—**a car, a dog, a fish, a girl, a house.**

Modifiers

A **modifier** is a word or phrase that describes, transforms, or provides additional information about a person, place, thing, or concept. Modifiers are often adjectives or adverbs or are phrases that include adjectives or adverbs.

When including a modifier in a sentence, you should place the modifier closest to the word being modified. Even with that said, you will discover that there are often more than one way to include modifiers within the sentence.

*During the concert, the audience applauded **loudly**.*
*During the concert, the audience **loudly** applauded.*

When a modifier is incorrectly placed within a sentence, this is an error called a **misplaced modifier.**

*The instructor **almost** failed the entire class. [Incorrect]*
*The instructor failed **almost** the entire class. [Correct]*
*Angelic **nearly** answered every question on the exam. [Incorrect]*
*Angelic answered **nearly** every question on the exam. [Correct]*

A **dangling modifier** is a phrase or dependent clause whose subject and verb are not stated but implied [elliptical clause]. Dangling modifiers are often placed at the beginning of sentences.

***Born into a large family**, it is difficult to adjust to solitude.*

The modifier above—born into a large family—does not modifier any part of the independent clause. The modifier is a reference to an unidentified person. Therefore, the modifier is dangling. The sentence fails to reveal who was born into a large family. There are a variety of ways to correct this sentence:

*Due to the fact that I was **born into a large family**, it is difficult to adjust to solitude.*

*Because I was **born into a large family**, it is difficult to adjust to solitude.*

***Born into a large family**, I had a difficult time adjusting to solitude.*

ADJECTIVES AND ADVERBS ASSIGNMENT

Print an updated copy of your essay. Circle all the adjectives and underline all of the adverbs in the composition. Verify that you have used the adverbs and adjectives correctly. If you made any adjective and adverb errors, use the editing marks on page 70 to make the appropriate changes to your composition. Be sure to make the changes on the electronic version of your essay stored on your jump drive.

Exercise: Adjectives and Adverbs I

Direction: Identify the correct adjective or adverb for each sentence.

1. Jessica held her friend (tight, tightly) as she told him the news about his father.
2. Despite her injuries, she is feeling (good, well).
3. The search committee was (careful, carefully) in their assessment of the applicants.
4. Mr. Johnson and Mr. Murphy (prematurely, premature) initiated a corporate merger with a new company.
5. The muscle cream smells surprisingly (well, good).
6. Despite her reluctance, she did a (well, good) job on the project.
7. Audrey, Amber, and I have decided to (quick, quickly) get rid of the rest of the product.
8. Keon is (slow, slowly) becoming one of the most respected players on the court.
9. Nadia's family looked (sad, sadly) when she told them her news.
10. The wind is (awful, awfully) strong.

Exercise: Adjectives and Adverbs II

Directions: Identify the correct adjective or adverb for each sentence.

1. The director of the council is (an, a) official member of the National Association for the Advancement of Colored People.
2. Gary's (general, generally) presence commands attention.
3. The refrigerator is open; close it (correct, correctly).
4. University of South Florida awarded the Chief Executive Officer of the nonprofit (an, a) Honorary Doctorate.
5. He is not a slow learner. He learns quit (quick, quickly).
6. Speak (quietly, quiet) only to your neighbor so you do not disturb anyone.
7. She is (quicker, more quick) than her competitor.
8. Although Jennifer was suspended for fighting, she is a (good, well) student.
9. He is having a (difficulty, difficult) time comprehending the new math equation.
10. <u>The Lovely Bones</u> is a mystery told by the dead victim. Although it sounds (strangely, strange), the novel is wonderful.

Modifiers: Exercise I

Directions: Carefully read each sentence and rewrite the sentence eliminating any misplaced or dangling modifiers. Write "correct" if there are not errors.

1. Upon reading the article, the mind was changed.
2. The student uncovered the fossil in the dirt carefully.
3. The agent interrogated the murder suspect before releasing him intensely.
4. The man chose the small Labrador with the large red hat from the dog pound.
5. Raised in New York, the rural life was not pleasing.
6. I was extremely tired from all the physical exercise.
7. To improve his time, the race was run again.
8. With little knowledge of him, it was hard to accept the blind date.
9. Without a proper description, finding the suspect will be difficult.
10. The young girl was hit by her brother's bicycle in a short skirt.

CHAPTER 29

PRONOUN AND ANTECEDENT AGREEMENT

Andrew and Amanda purchased a two-bedroom loft in downtown Jacksonville. Andrew and Amanda will move in on the first of next month. Andrew and Amanda have scheduled a moving van.

What is wrong with the above passage? For one, consistently restating "Andrew and Amanda" is awkward. Using pronouns is an effective way to rename nouns. **Pronouns** are used as substitutes or replacements for nouns, noun phrases, or other pronouns. An **antecedent** is a word or phrase the pronoun has replaced.

Now, look at the same passage with pronoun substitutions.

Andrew and Amanda purchased a two-bedroom loft in downtown Jacksonville. They will move in on the first of next month. They have scheduled a moving van.

"**They**" is the pronoun. "**Andrew and Amanda**" is the antecedent.

PRONOUN CASE

Pronouns are a big part of the language used in standard American English. Pronouns function as subjects, objects, and possessives. It is important to use the appropriate pronoun case.

Subjective	Objective	Possessive
I	Me	my/mine
We	Us	our/ours
You	You	your/yours
he/she/it	Him/her/it	his/her/hers/its
They	Them	their/theirs
who/whoever	whom/whomever	Whose

Examine the use of pronouns in the sentences below.

John and *I* have become distant from *her*, but the problem is *hers*, not *ours*.

During *our* presentation, *he* decided to award a prize to *whoever* could correctly answer the trivia questions.

Who ate the last cookie? To *whom* do *I* need to speak with?

Who or Whom

Who and **whoever** are subjective pronouns. Therefore, you would use the appropriate version of these pronouns in the subject. If the pronoun is not a part of the subject, you would use **whom** or **whomever**. These pronouns are objective. Although the distinction is easy to remember, most people confuse the subjective and the objective cases, and they do not know when to use who or whom.

To determine the correct pronoun case, it may prove beneficial to re-arrange the sentence for clarity.

Troy Steward is the man *whom* I met in the market. [I met him in the market]
Him is objective; therefore, the objective form *whom* is appropriate.

I am not sure *who* will attend the press conference. [He will attend the press conference.] *He [or she]* is the subject case; therefore, the subject form who is appropriate.

To whom do I owe my gratitude? [I owe my gratitude to him.]
Him is the objective form of he; therefore, *whom* is appropriate.

Who is riding with us? [He is riding with us.]
He is the subjective form; therefore, *who* is appropriate.

Pronoun and Antecedent Agreement

The pronoun and the antecedent must agree in number and gender. Examine the following examples:

1. **A parent** is responsible for **their** child.—INCORRECT
2. **Ms. Jenkins** invited **his** coworkers to **his** piano recital.—INCORRECT

In the first sentence, the antecedent "parent" is singular in number, and the gender is undefined. The pronoun "their" is plural.

In the second sentence, the antecedent "Ms. Jenkins" is singular in number and female in gender. The pronoun "his" is singular, but "his" is male.

When the pronoun and antecedent do not agree in number, the syntactical structure of the sentence is flawed. Examine the corrections of the above sentences.

A parent is responsible for **his** child.—CORRECT

The antecedent "parent" is singular in number, and the gender is undefined. The pronoun "his" is singular. *When the gender is undefined, use the male gender. Using "he or she" or "his or her" is awkward.*

Ms. Jenkins invited her coworkers to **her** piano recital.—CORRECT

The antecedent "Ms. Jenkins" is singular in number and female in gender. The pronoun "her" is singular and female.

Remember, certain indefinite pronouns are always singular, some can be singular or plural, and some are always plural.

Always Singular	Anyone, another, anything, each, either, no on, neither, nobody, one, someone, somebody
Either plural or singular	All, most, none, some
Always Plural	Both, few, many, several

Examine how indefinite pronouns affect pronoun antecedent agreement.

Anyone can purchase the equipment if **he** has the money.
Most of the parents have picked up **their** children.

PRONOUN AND ANTECEDENT AGREEMENT ASSIGNMENT

Print an additional copy of your essay. Examine each sentence of your essay for pronoun case and pronoun and antecedent agreement errors. Use the editing mark on page 70 to make the appropriate changes to your composition. Be sure to make the changes on the electronic version of your essay stored on your jump drive.

Exercise: Pronoun Case I

Directions: Carefully read each sentence. Identify the correct pronoun case for each sentence.

1. Adam and (he, him) were among the first participants to arrive.
2. During the concert, the singer threw his hat to (she, her).

3. John is the student (who, whom) I was unable convince about possible inaccuracies in American history.
4. (We, Our) party was an unexpected disappointment.
5. With (whom, who) will you come to the party?
6. (Who, Whom) will you bring to the party?
7. The father wanted to order his daughter a birthday cake, but he did not know (her, she) age.
8. The man asked the sale agent for a recommendation for (his, him) son's first car.
9. This is not (her, she) first time away from home.
10. Men and women engage in conversation quite differently. (They, Their) differences can cause miscommunication.

Exercise: Pronoun and Antecedent Agreement I

Directions: Carefully read each sentence. Some of the sentences have pronoun and antecedent agreement errors; some of them do not. Rewrite the incorrect sentences, correcting the pronoun and antecedent errors.

1. Each teammate must ensure their locker has been secured.
2. All teachers have a responsibility to each of hers students.
3. Everyone needs to take a copy of their physical to the health official.
4. One of the students has been selected to present their proposal to the faculty.
5. If Angela wants to win the game, she has to know the rules.
6. Although William is going to the reception, they have to leave early.
7. Someone left their keys on the counter.
8. Because Nia's painting has been selecting, they will receive a cash reward.
9. Monica and Tamara found her mother's locket.
10. The faculty and staff at Edward Waters College has selected a representative.

Exercise: Pronoun and Antecedent Agreement II

Directions: Read the paragraph below. Select the correct pronoun to agree with the corresponding antecedent.

Euthanasia thwarts a person's fight for life. It is common for an individual to experience shock when (he, they) is initially diagnosed with a terminal illness. In such a state, everyone is not able to think rationally about (their, his) options. A person who would initially decide to be euthanized could change (his, their) mind once the shock wears off. With encouragement and support, (they, he) may also decide to fight for (his, their) life. In addition to the shock, a terminally ill patient may receive bad advice. Unfortunately, not everyone has another person's best interest at heart.

This is even the case in some families. A patient's family could encourage (him, them) to avoid the pain, but the family members' true motives may be (her, their) own financial gain. The patient is too vulnerable. Most importantly, people must realize that God has a plan for everyone's life. A "terminal illness" could be a way for God to test a person's faith. Many people have been cured from terminal illnesses, and these cases are documented. Knowing such should give each person hope, for (he, they) too could overcome (his, their) condition.

CHAPTER 30

COMMONLY CONFUSED WORDS

American English includes many sets of words that sound and look alike, and it can prove difficult to know when to use which word. **Homophones** are words that sound alike but have different meanings. **Homonyms** are words that look similar but have different meanings. **Homographs** are words that have the same spelling, but the words can differ in pronunciation and differ in meaning. Many writers confuse a variety of word sets. The table below reflects a list of many [not all] commonly confused words.

Are (verb)—to be **Our** (pronoun)—possessive form of "we" **Hour** (noun)—a 60-minute time period	**Altogether**—entirely **All together** (two words)—gathered in one place	**Bear** (noun)—animal (verb)—to hold up/support (verb) to endure **Bare** (adjective)—nude/without covering (verb)—to reveal	**Brake** (verb)—to slow (noun)—a device used to slow a vehicle **Break** (verb)—to smash, shatter (noun)—an interruption (noun)—a fracture (noun)—an escape/dash

Alter (verb)—to change **Altar** (noun)—a place of worship/sacrifice	**A part** (two words)—to be joined with **Apart** (adverb)—to be separated	**Because** (conjunction)—for the reason that **Cause** (noun)—an effect/consequence		
Are (verb)—to be **Our** (pronoun)—possessive form of "we" **Hour** (noun)—a 60-minute time period	**Altogether**-- entirely **All together** (two words)—gathered in one place	**Bear** (noun)—animal (verb)—to hold up/support (verb) to endure **Bare** (adjective)—nude/without covering (verb)—to reveal		
By (preposition)—near **Bye** –used as a salutation when leaving someone "bye-bye" **Buy** (verb)—to purchase	**Capital** (noun)—city of government, upper case letter, top of a column, money or property **Capitol** (noun)—main government building [capitalize when referring to U.S. Congress meeting location]	**Council** (noun)—an administrative body **Counsel** (noun)- advice or guidance (verb)—to give advice or guidance	**Compliment** (noun)—a positive expression given to a person **Complement** (noun)—a thing added to something to enhance	
Coarse (adjective) rough **Course** (noun)—a series of actions/events, a class, conduct (verb)—to issue from	**Credible** (adjective) believable, convincing **Creditable** (adjective) deserving acknowledgement or praise	**Desert** (noun)—dry, waterless area of land **Dessert** (noun)—a sweet food	**Farther** (adverb)—at a greater point or distance **Further** (verb)—to advance (adjective)—additional	
Formally (adverb) officially, properly **Formerly** (adverb) earlier	**Forth** (adverb) advance out into view **Fourth** (adverb) after third	**Grate** (verb) to shred, to annoy **Great** (adjective) wonderful, impressive, large,	**Hear** (verb) to listen, to receive sound **Here** (adverb) at this point in time or location	

Commonly Confused Words

Hole (noun) gap, break, cavity **Whole** (adjective) entire, total, in one piece	**Hoe** (verb) to tidy, to weed, to pick over (noun) a garden tool **Whore** (noun) a prostitute	**Its** (pronoun) possessive of it **It's** (actually two words) contraction for "It is"	**Know** (verb) be familiar with **No** (noun) rejection opposite of "yes" **Now** (adverb) currently, at this time
Knew (verb) past tense of "know" **New** (adjective) latest, modern—opposite of "old"	**Later** (adverb) afterward, in a while **Latter** (adjective) last, final **Ladder** (noun) steps, object used to obtain higher ground, ranking	**Lead** [*sounds like* "leed"] (verb) to guide or begin [leed] (noun) clue [led] (noun) think marking substance found in pencils **Led** (verb) past tense of "lead"	**Lie** (verb) to recline, to stretch out **Lay** (verb) to place or to put something down
Passed (verb)—to go by, to get ahead of past tense of "pass" **Past** (noun) history (adjective) earlier, gone	**Peace** (noun) calm, concord, tranquility **Piece** (noun)- bit, slice, portion	**Proceed** (verb) to go on, carry on, continue **Precede** (verb) to head, to lead, to go before	**Principal** (noun) head of the school (adjective) major, primary **Principle** (noun)— code, standard, belief
	Pore (noun) hole, minute opening **Pour** (verb) tip, empty, dispense, cause to flow **Poor** (adjective) needy		
Quite (adverb) very, to a certain extent **Quit** (verb) to give up, to leave **Quiet** (adjective) hushed, gentle (verb) to calm down, to silence	**Sea** (noun) large body of water, ocean **See** (verb) to set eyes on, to observe (verb) to understand	**Site** (noun) place, location (verb) to situate **Sight** (noun) vision (verb) to notice **Cite** (verb) to quote, to refer to	**Than** (conjunction) used to indicate difference **Then** (adverb) next, after than, consequently
There (adverb) in that matter, respect, location **Their** (adjective) possessive of "they" **They're** (two words) contraction for "they are"	**Through** (adverb) from end to end (preposition) in the course of (adjective) finished **Threw** (verb) past tense of "throw" ***Thru** (non word)	**Though** (adverb) however (conjunction) even if, despite the fact that **Thorough** (adjective) methodical, systematic, careful, complete	**To** (preposition) in the direction of, toward **Too** (adverb) as well as, also, (adverb) excessively **Two** (adjective) the number after one

Weak (adjective) feeble, fragile, not strong Week (noun) seven day period	Weather (noun) climate (verb) endure Whether (conjunction) if	Were (verb) past plural tense of is "to be" Where (adverb) location, at a place We're (two words) contraction for "we are"	Whose (adjective) possessive of whom or which Who's (two words) contraction for "who is"

COMMONLY CONFUSED WORDS ASSIGNMENT

Print an additional copy of your essay. Examine each sentence of your essay incorrect use of commonly confused words. Use the editing marks on page 70 to make the appropriate changes to your composition. Be sure to make the changes on the electronic version of your essay stored on your jump drive.

Exercise: Commonly Confused Words I

Directions: Identify the correct word for each sentence.

1. Due to (weather, whether), I was unable to see (weather, whether) Ms. Johnson's son would make the winning touchdown.
2. This (weak, week), the team will compete (for, four) the championship.
3. The dead (foul, fowl) produced a (foul, fowl) odor.
4. (Their, there) conflict with Mr. Johnson has lasted for far (to, too) long.
5. Jasmine is much more capable (than, then) Sarah, but Sarah was promoted.
6. During the (passed, past) six weeks, I have learned more about history (then, than) I have learned in my (whole, hole) life.
7. The (principle, principal) (lead, led) the parents around the school during the tour.
8. The baker cut a large (piece, peace) of toffee, but I was not able to (break, brake) it.
9. (Hour, Our) (new, knew) friend is a (great, grate) hostess.
10. She planned to (by, buy) a locket, but she had to (alter, altar) her plan.

Exercise: Commonly Confused Words II

Directions: Identify the correct words.

There are numerous activities that I enjoy, (butt, but) my favorite hobby is playing football. My (whole, hole) family enjoys football. Even though my mother thought it was a (course, coarse) game, we used to watch games (all together, altogether). We would always argue about (whose, who's) team would win. I also watched my older brothers play football, so I began playing football at an early age. They (where, were) my inspiration. However, watching football is even better than playing it (cause, because) you can learn moves or see how you can improve (you're, your) skills. I still watch football every (week, weak) during football season. Football is also beneficial (too, to) my health. I am physically fit and football keeps me that way. Although I have many hobbies, football is my favorite hobby.

CHAPTER 31

TRANSITIONS

A **transition [transitional device]** is a word or phrase that signifies the move from one idea to the next. Transitions also identify the relationship of information or ideas.

Think of the ideas in your composition as islands, and think of transitions as bridges. To get from one idea [island] to the next idea, you need a transition [bridge].

ANSWER: An effective writer uses transitions so his ideas flow from one to the next. This will allow the reader to better understand the author's thoughts, and the reader will also know when one idea ends and a new idea begins.

There are several types of transitions, and you would use the appropriate transition based on the relationship of the information.

Why does an effective composition include transitions?

Relationship	Transitions
Time	after, afterward, at last, before, currently, during, earlier, immediately, later, meanwhile, now, recently, simultaneously, subsequently, then
Examples	for example, for instance, namely, specifically, to illustrate

Writing for Rights, pages 139–142.
Copyright © 2025 *Patrice W. Glenn*
Published under exclusive licence by Emerald Publishing Limited
ISBNs: 978-1-83708-490-6 HB, 978-1-83708-491-3 PB,
978-1-83708-492-0 EPDF, 978-1-83708-493-7 EPUB

Relationship	Transitions
Cause/effect	accordingly, consequently, hence, so, therefore, thus
Adding to	additionally, again, also, and, as well, besides, equally important, further, furthermore, in addition, moreover, then
Place/position	above, adjacent, below, beyond, here, in front, in back, nearby, there
Emphasis	even, indeed, in fact, of course, truly
Sequence/chronological order	first, second, third, ... next, then, finally
Exception/contrasting Ideas	but, however, in spite of, on the one hand ... on the other hand, nevertheless, nonetheless, notwithstanding, in contrast, on the contrary, still, yet
Similarity/comparing ideas	also, in the same way, just as ... so too, likewise, similarly
Concluding/to summarize	finally, in a word, in brief, in conclusion, in the end, in the final analysis, on the whole, thus, to conclude, to summarize, in sum, in summary

Use transitions between sentences, paragraphs, and ideas.

TRANSITIONS ASSIGNMENT

Print an additional copy of your essay. Carefully examine the relationship among sentences and paragraphs in your essay. Include the appropriate transitions to reveal the relationship of the sentences and the paragraphs. Each sentences does not necessarily need a transition. Use the editing marks on page 70 to make the appropriate changes to your composition. Be sure to make the changes on the electronic version of your essay stored on your jump drive.

Exercise: Transitions I

Directions: Insert the best transition to complete each sentence.

1. Health Care Unlimited will pay forty percent of the medical bill; _____, the policy holder must pay a deductible.

    similarly *for example* *however*

2. The university increased their tuition. _____, many students did not return this semester.

    As a result *In brief* *Subsequently*

3. First, Mrs. Jones must submit the correct paperwork. _____ she has to schedule an appointment.

   Adjacent   *Next*   *Also*

4. On one hand, the detective thinks he should follow the suspect. _____, he may need to wait for backup.

 In the same way   *Of course*   *On the other hand*

5. Asia knew she was going to receive the award. _____, she was so confident, she prepared an acceptance speech.

   In fact   *For example*   *Further*

6. Dr. Parker-Graham enjoyed her stay at the Gaylord Opryland Resort; _____, she has planned another trip during the summer.

  additionally   *therefore*   *however*

7. Many men view baking as a skill for women. _____, women view car repair as a skill for men.

   Likewise   *Additionally*   *In a word*

8. You have allowed us to use this information; _____, we cannot be sure how it will be used.

   but   *similarly*   *in fact*

9. The organization increased the membership requirements. _____, the changes will not accept existing members.

   Meanwhile   *However*   *Therefore*

10. Monique worked diligently to complete the assignment. She _____ completed the task on the eve of the due date.

   finally   *ultimately*   *last*

Exercise: Transitions II

Directions: Insert transitions in the blanks to link the ideas and make this composition more coherent.

Although many people do not explore the concept of management on a daily basis, if asked to explain the concept, most would not hesitate in providing their idea of management and the role of a manager. _____ the responses would probably be as distinctive in number as the number of persons questioned. _____ there would be some common occurrences and common threads, _____ each person's idea of management and what makes a strong manager would probably stem from his own experiences and desires. _____ lay persons may not delve into the idea of management, most companies work fervently to make sure their customers are receiving the best service or product they can receive. Whether it is a child's education or a new car, quality is what the customer expects, _____quality is at the heart of each organization's mission.

Exercise: Transitions III

Directions: Insert transitions to link the ideas and make this composition more coherent.

A leader sets goals. It is important to begin with the end in mind. When a leader lacks vision, those he is leading are left without direction and they fail to fill a common mission. A leader leads by example by showing his constituents the right way to do things. Leaders demonstrate leadership through effective time management. Time is a force we cannot control. We can use time to our advantage. Honesty is a characteristic of a good leader. An effective leader should not lie if he wants the trust of his followers. A leader has to be honest unless he wants to lie to him.

CHAPTER 32

DOUBLE NEGATIVES

You may have heard the phrase, "opposites attract." When referring to the science of magnets [and some say the science of physical attractions], such is true. Negatives attract positives. A positive and a positive will repel, and a negative and a negative will repel.

When a writer wants to express the opposite of a positive expression, he must use a negative word or phrase.

I want to go to the banquet. [positive construction]

I do <u>not</u> want to go to the banquet. [negative construction]

The following is a list of negative words. Using the words in a sentence will take the sentence negative.

NEGATIVE WORDS

no	not*
none	no one
nobody	nothing

neither
hardly
scarcely
nowhere
never
barely

*Using not with any verb makes the verb negative. Using a contraction form of not with a verb is also negative: can't[cannot], won't [will not], shouldn't [shouldn't].

A **double negative** is the incorrect use of two negative words or phrases within the same sentence. Using two negatives is a grammatical error. When two negatives are used, they contradict each other and create a positive. Therefore, when you want to express a negative, use only one negative word in a sentence.

Negative + **Negative = Positive**	Sheila cannot see no one she knows in the crowd.	**Incorrect.** *This is a double negative. This sentence actually means Sheila can see someone she knows.*
Positive construction One negative	Sheila can see no one she knows in the crowd.	**Correct**
Positive construction One negative	Sheila cannot see anyone she knows in the crowd.	**Correct**

DOUBLE NEGATIVES ASSIGNMENT

Print an additional copy of your essay. Examine each sentence of your essay for double negatives. Use the editing mark son page 70 to make the appropriate changes to your composition. Be sure to make the changes on the electronic version of your essay stored on your jump drive.

Double Negatives I

Directions: Carefully read each sentence. Rewrite any sentences to eliminate double negatives.

1. Despite his conjecture, there is not nothing going on between the two of us.
2. I did not invite no one from my office to the party; I am tired of my coworkers.
3. Trey does not never find any comfort in the alcohol he drinks.
4. Even though I received many presents, I did not like none of them.
5. DeAllen cannot scarcely contain himself when he watches wrestling.

6. Johnny didn't hear nothing unusual.
7. She was so excited, she could not barely contain herself.
8. Although they received specific instruction from their teacher, the students did not read no books.
9. There is hardly no snow fall in Florida.
10. There was no need to conduct an investigation because the suspect did not hardly oppose to his guilt.

Double Negatives II

Directions: Carefully read the paragraph. Rewrite the passage to eliminate double negatives.

Euthanasia is not a positive thing for no one; it thwarts a person's fight for life. First, most people experience shock when they are initially diagnosed with a terminal illness. In such a state, no one is not able to think rationally about his options. A person who would initially decide to be euthanized could change his mind once the shock where's off. With encouragement and support, he may also decide to fight for his life. In addition to the shock, terminally ill patients may receive bad advice. Unfortunately, not everyone hardly has another person's best interest at heart. This is even the case in some families. A patient's family could encourage him to avoid the pain, but the family member may not barely care about the patient. The patient is too vulnerable to make such a permanent decision. Most importantly, people must realize that God has a plan for everyone's life. A terminal illness could be a way for God to test a person's faith. Many patients have overcome their illness even though the physician said there was no way they would not. Most people know someone who has been cured from terminal illnesses, and these cases are documented. Knowing such should give every person hope, for they too could overcome their condition.

This page marks the end of this grammar section.

Revisit the previous section as a reference.

CHAPTER 33

SENTENCE VARIETY

One characteristic of quality compositions, no matter the purpose, is sentence variety. Variety in type and variety in length are included in this context. If you Google "types of sentences," your search will likely yield four common sentence types: (1) simple, (2) compound, (3) complex, and (4) compound-complex. If not the aforementioned types, four others will result: (1) declarative (basic sentence), (2) imperative (command), (3) interrogative (question), and (4) exclamatory (strong, emotional statement).

While it may have been a while since you encountered these terminology-heavy categories, the truth is that few people read your words and consciously think, "Ah, this is an interrogative sentence." Instead, they react to the clarity and flow of your writing with responses like, "This doesn't make sense," "Huh?" or "What's the author trying to covey?" being more common.

Structure and Function

Understanding sentence types, both in structure and function, isn't about demonstrating your grammar expertise, which you have recently cultivated. It's about constructing a clear, compelling, and effective composition. Variety in sentence structure—simple, compound, complex, and compound-complex—is an important characteristic of an effective composition. Similarly, it is important to con-

Writing for Rights, pages 147–149.
Copyright © 2025 *Patrice W. Glenn*
Published under exclusive licence by Emerald Publishing Limited
ISBNs: 978-1-83708-490-6 HB, 978-1-83708-491-3 PB,
978-1-83708-492-0 EPDF, 978-1-83708-493-7 EPUB

sider the different functions of sentences: asking questions, making a command, expressing emotional ideals, and so on. Therefore, your sentences need to vary.

Using Sentences

If you are like me, you this commentary may lead you to ask a question. *How do I know which type of sentence to use?* The following tips should help you:

1. Use **compound sentences to combine two closely related sentences**. Demonstrate cause and effect, definition, and such connections through sentence combining.
   EXAMPLES:
   – *The technician had little knowledge about unmanned aerial vehicles, but he was both willing to learn and diligent.*
        (Note the relationship between these two statements.)
   – Unmanned aerial vehicles are often referred to as UAVs; these pilotless aircrafts are also called drones.
        (Note how the second sentence provides further explanation of the UAVs).
2. Use **simple sentences for emphasis**. Often, we like to insert exclamation marks; do not do so. Instead, merely formulate a short, simple sentence. (By the way, exclamation marks should be used only in dialogue in a narrative.)
   EXAMPLE:
   – After twelve years working in tandem, Jacob discovered a plan of betrayal that directly involved his partner, John. Initially, Jacob did not want to believe it; however, after conclusive evidence, he had no choice. *Jacob was hurt.*
        (Note the impact of the final sentence.)
3. Use **interrogative sentences (questions) to address the reader and capture his or her attention about the topic.**
   EXAMPLE:
   – Toxic leadership negatively impacts an organization's culture. The affects are likely to linger from time beyond the leader's involvement. *What, then, can be done to correct a toxic organizational structure?*
4. Avoid **imperative sentences in academic writing**. Although it may seem appropriate, stay away from this practice. These types of sentences can backfire.
   EXAMPLES:
   – You should not support gun control.
     • (This sentence uses the second person pronoun "you." Third person is the most appropriate writing tense, so stay away from second person perspective [you, your, yourself]. Provide labels for this arbitrary "you." Ask yourself, who is

"you"?) Here is a revision, "Parents should not support gun control." In this version, "parents" replaces "you," and the sentence moves from an imperative to a declaration for a specific group.
- Do not do drugs.
  - (As writers, we want to move the reader into action by presenting a logical, emotional, and credible composition that is supported by fact-based information). We do not want to provide directives. Again, stay away from imperative statements.

Writing goes beyond how words are arranged on a page. It is also about creating an experience for the reader by interweaving ideas and the emotions they evoke with the reader.

Sentence variety infuses a composition with rhythm, depth, and impact. By weaving together simple, compound, complex, and compound-complex sentences and questions, you create a dynamic flow that keeps the reader engaged and eager to journey through your words.

CHAPTER 34

QUALITY CONTENT

Drawing upon the wisdom of professionals and scholars can significantly enhance the impact of any written work. These individuals are often experts in their fields, possessing a wealth of knowledge and experience. Therefore, when you reference their insights, it lends credibility and authority to your work. Readers are more likely to trust and value information that comes from reputable sources.

A quote represents the precise reiteration of someone else's words or perspectives. When engaging in the research and composition of papers, it becomes imperative to incorporate the insights of experts and scholars. Quotes offer depth and breadth of knowledge that can enrich your writing by providing nuanced perspectives, historical context, and up-to-date information. This depth adds substance and sophistication to your work. Thus, understanding the correct way to integrate quotes into your composition is vital.

The way you include quotes largely depends on the specific writing style you are using. Irrespective of the style that you use, certain consistent methods exist for formatting both short and long quotations.

Short and Long Quotes

The length of the quote determines the formatting. Generally, **short quotes** consist of 39 words or less or fit on three or less typed lines. Short quotes are included among the commentary of the composition. Short quotes are enclosed in quotation marks. Examine the example below. The quote is bolded.

> According to The American Federation of Teachers (2007), "**there is no nation that has been or is close to meeting the kind of standards that has been set by NCLB**" (para. 5).

Long quotes consist of 40 or more words. Long quotes are not enclosed within quotation marks. When a writer includes a long quote in his composition, he must set the quote apart from the rest of the text. He must return to the next line and indent the left margin 5–7 spaces or one tab space of each line. Examine the example below. The quoted information is bolded.

> Funds allotted by NCLB for school districts never make it to the schools because of all the cuts taking place at the state level. Thus, the nation's neediest children have been chronically under-funded. According to The National Education Association (2007),
>
> **The nation's schools received $9.8 billion less than they would have if No Child Left Behind was funded at the level Congress promised in the law and under President Bush's proposed budget for 2006, the nation's schools will receive $12 billion less than what Congress authorized when the federal law was enacted.** (para. 3)
>
> Washington lawmakers have not done their legal duty of paying for the rules and regulations that is imposed on this nation's schools.

Notice that there are no quotations marks around the quote.

Including Signal Phrases

In the preceding long quote, the writer alerts the reader to the source of the quote. He writes, *"According to the National Education Association"*.

This phrase lets the reader know made the statement. A **signal phrase** is a phrase that indicates who made the original statement. Signal phrases are important because they alert the reader to the original source of the information; signal phrases also give the original author credit for making the statement. *According to* is among the most common signal phrases used in academic writing. As in, *According to Felix Adler,* "**To care for anyone else enough to make their problems one's own, is ever the beginning of one's real ethical development.**"

The signal phrase indicates that Felix Adler is the person who made the statement. The beginning of the Adler's comment is marked by a quotation mark and the end of the quote is also signified by a quotation mark. Signal phrases are used with both long and short quotes, as well as with paraphrases. Paraphrases are introduced later in this chapter.

For now, examine some common signal phrases, their uses, and examples.

Signal Phrase	Use	Example
According to	Used to introduce a source's viewpoint or information	According to Smith, climate change is a pressing global concern.
In the words of	Used to directly attribute a quote or idea to its source	In the words of Martin Luther King Jr., "I have a dream that one day..."
As stated by	Similar to "according to," it introduces a source's statement	As stated by the World Health Organization, vaccination is crucial for public health.
Argues that	Signals the author's position or argument	Smith argues that "renewable energy sources are the key to reducing carbon emissions."
Research shows	Indicates that there is evidence supporting the statement	Research shows that exercise can have a positive impact on mental health.
Contends that	Indicates a strong assertion or viewpoint	Jones contends that "...access to quality education is a fundamental human right."

Incorporating signal phrases like the examples provided serves as a crucial technique to enhance the flow and coherence of your text. These phrases act as signposts, guiding your readers through the intricate terrain of your arguments and ideas. They provide essential context and attribution; they also offer clarity to your composition.

Without signal phrases, quotes, as well as paraphrased content, may appear disconnected, disjointed, or even out of place. Readers might find it challenging to discern the source of the material or even its relevance to your discussion. This lack of clarity can disrupt the smooth progression of your ideas and can leave your reader puzzled and less engaged.

Paraphrasing

Let's be frank. Sometimes, the previous author's use of language just does not have the same tone or style as your original writing. In some instances, your writing style differs so dramatically from that of previous writers it becomes necessary to rephrase the author's ideas to fit the tone of your composition.

This is where paraphrasing comes in. Paraphrasing is the art of rewriting someone else's words or ideas in your own unique voice and style. The use of paraphrasing allows you to maintain the integrity of the original idea while infusing the previous author's content with your voice.

Let's examine both quoting and paraphrasing in action.

Here is our quote, "Injustice anywhere is a threat to justice everywhere." These words were spoken by Dr. Martin Luther King Jr.

If the tone of King's words aligns with the style of your writing, you would merely include an appropriate signal phrase to introduce the quote. In the sample provided, the quote and signal phrase are in both font:

> **According to Dr. Martin Luther King Jr., "Injustice anywhere is a threat to justice everywhere."** These profound words remind us that the fight for justice knows no borders and that when we witness injustice, whether in our own communities or around the world, it is our moral duty to stand up and speak out. King's message resonates as a timeless call to action, urging us to be vigilant in our pursuit of a more equitable and just society for all.

Notice that King's words are placed within quotation marks. In addition to the signal phrase, this formatting alerts the reader that these words belong to someone else, not the present writer.

Let's look at the same content but using paraphrasing to incorporate King's ideas. As with the previous passage, the paraphrased information and an appropriate signal phrase are in bold font.

> **In his renowned speech, Dr. Martin Luther King Jr. emphasized that unfairness in one place poses a risk to justice in all places.** This powerful message reminds us that the fight for justice knows no borders and that when we witness injustice, whether in our own communities or around the world, it is our moral duty to stand up and speak out. King's message resonates as a timeless call to action, urging us to be vigilant in our pursuit of a more equitable and just society for all.

It is longer to wonder when you quote and when you should paraphrase. While tone and style are at the heart of the answer, it depends on your writing's purpose. The use of quotes can be more assertive. Thus, use quotes when you want to capture the author's exact words or when those words are so powerful that changing them would weaken the impact. Paraphrase when you want to incorporate the idea into your own compositing, adding your voice to the conversation.

QUALITY CONTENT WRITING ASSIGNMENT:

To enhance your writing skills, effectively integrate quotes and paraphrases into an existing composition to reinforce your arguments and present diverse perspectives.

1. **Select a composition:** Choose an existing piece of writing that you have previously worked on. Ensure the composition is at least one page and length and focuses on a specific topic or argument.

2. **Identify opportunities:** Review your composition and identify areas where the inclusion of quotes and paraphrases can strengthen your arguments, provide evidence, or offer different viewpoints. Consider how these textual elements can enhance the overall quality and clarity of your work.
3. **Select a quote:** Find a relevant quote from a reputable source that supports or adds depths to a point you're making in your composition. Make sure to introduce the quote with a signal phrase, place it within quotation marks, and provide an appropriate citation.
4. **Provide a paraphrase:** Identify a section of your composition where paraphrasing could be beneficial. Take a passage from your own writing or from another source related to your topic and rephrase it in your ow words. Ensure the paraphrase retains the original meaning and context while adopting your writing style.
5. **Revise and proofread:** Make sure the quote and paraphrase were seamlessly integrated into your composition. Pay attention to the flow and coherence of your writing, ensuring that the quote and paraphrase fit naturally within the context of your work. Make any necessary revisions to improve clarity and coherence.
6. **Reflection and significance:** In a separate composition, write a brief explanation of why you chose to include it and how it enhances your composition. Discuss how these textual elements contribute to the overall message or argument you're conveying.

CHAPTER 35

USING NUMBERS

In the realm of writing, words compel readers to action. Yet, behind the impact of words lies the world of numbers. Numbers play a crucial role in writing, providing structure, context, and precision to our words and ideas.

Consider the opening of a novel, where the chapter number sets the stage for what's coming. It tells us where we are in the storying guiding our expectations and preparing us for the narrative journey ahead. Numbers also lend credibility to our arguments, providing statistics, percentages, and figures that support our claims and weight to our persuasion.

In technical writing, numbers quantify data, measurements, and outcomes. They transform abstract concepts into tangible realities, making complex information more accessible to the reader. From scientific research papers to financial reports, numbers are the backbone of clarity and accuracy.

Even in creative writing, numbers can be a source of inspiration. A countdown creates suspense, a date marks an important moment in time, and a sequence of numbers can form a cryptic code in a mystery novel. Numbers can add layers of meaning, hidden messages, or a sense of urgency to your composition.

Ultimately, numbers and words are partners in effective communication. However, it is important to adhere to key guidelines to ensure clarity, consistency, and readability:

1. **Begin with words, not numbers:** When expressing numbers at the beginning of a sentence, it's generally best to spell out the words. For instance, write *"Three hundred participants attend the event,"* rather than "300 participants attended the event."
2. **Use words for zero through nine:** Spell out numbers from zero through nine, as they are typically expressed as words in most writing contexts. For example, *"There were five new research findings."*
3. **Use numbers for multiple-word numbers:** For numbers that consist of two or more words, it is generally more practical to use numerals. For instance, *"The study reported 53 cases of infection."*
4. **Use "amount" for non-countable items:** When referring to quantities of things that cannot be counted individually, such as grains of sand or water, use the word "amount." For instance, *the amount of sand on the beach was astounding."*
5. **Use "number" for countable items:** When referring to quantities of items that can be counted, such as people, cars, or books, use the word "number". For example, *"The number of participants in the study exceeded expectations."*
6. **Refer to writing format guidelines:** Depending on the writing format you are using (e.g., APA, MLA, Chicago), there may be specific rules for how to present numbers. It's essential to consult the guidelines of our chosen format to ensure consistency and compliance.

By following these guidelines, you can effectively navigate the world of writing numbers, ensuring that your compositions maintain consistency and readability while adhering to the specific requirements of your chose writing format.

CHAPTER 36

THE PROFOUND PROCESS OF PUBLISHING

When writing for rights, a profound process exists that serves as a transformative journey, leading us towards the creation of compositions that possess the power to inspire, motivate, and drive change. This process is a lot like assembling a puzzle, where each piece meticulously put in place contributes to the bigger picture of your composition. Within this framework, three key elements—grammar, revision, and proofreading—take center stage, functioning as our guiding lights toward crafting impactful compositions.

Grammar: The Foundation of Clarity

Grammar is the bedrock upon which your composition is built. It serves as the solid ground from which your ideas can soar. Just as social justice advocates rely on well-established principles to champion their causes, writers employ grammar as a tool to convey thoughts with precision and coherence. Grammar ensures that your sentences stand strong and that your messages are crystal clear.

To draft letters to senators, calls to action, or blogs that resonate with readers, you must wield grammar with intent. Every sentence should be grammatically sound, each verb tense should be consistent, and pronouns must navigate without confusion. Just as social justice thrives on clarity and transparency, your words must be impeccable conveyors of your message.

Revision: Crafting the Composition

Revision is where the true magic unfolds. It's the phase where you sculpt your composition into a powerful instrument of change. Much like social justice movements adapt to address evolving challenges, your writing must undergo transformation during the revision process. This is the juncture where your ideas take shape, your arguments gain potency, and your composition aligns with the social justice theme you seek to convey.

As you revise, consider the coherence of your argument. Are your ideas logically structured and seamlessly connected? Do your examples and evidence resonate with your social justice theme? The revision process is your opportunity to refine your narrative, ensuring that it not only engages reade4rs but also stirs their emotions, much like social justice causes ignite passion and inspire action.

Proofreading: The Final Flourish

Proofreading serves as the ultimate polish that elevates your composition. It is the stage where you meticulously comb through your work, correcting any lingering errors or inconsistencies.

During the proofreading stage, you hunt for typos, grammatical slip ups, and formatting glitches. Just as social justice advocates tirelessly work to rectify systematic injustices, you must be unwave4ring in your commitment to perfect your writing until it gleams with professional precision.

Very few advocates work alone; we need each other to advance change. Likewise, a mistake that far too many novice writers make is to go at the proofreading process alone. Professional authors have editors, so think how much more novice writers should rely on the support and assistance of peers who can help produce a publication-ready composition.

CHAPTER 37

A CHANGE IN OUR WRITING

Throughout this text, we have explored writing from a content development perspective as well as with consideration for sentence structure and grammar. We have also interjected ideas about the importance of voice and message when advocating for issues that impact communities and societies and those that seek justice.

The message throughout this text is that how we communicate through writing influences the impact of our messages. Our readers and audiences cannot be called to action if they cannot connect with and understand our message.

Early in the text, we shared a basic composition about empathy. The revised version of that passage considers the lessons learned throughout this text.

The Cry for Empathy: Our Society's Deafening Silence
In a world buzzing with technological marvels, artificial intelligence, and groundbreaking discoveries, there is one fundamental trait that seems to be slipping through our collective fingers—empathy. It's a word we hear often, a virtue we claim to cherish, yet its scarcity in our daily interactions is palpable. As we navigate an era marked by rapid change and divisiveness, the clarion call for empathy in our society grows louder and more urgent than ever.

According to President Barack Obama, "learning to stand in somebody else's shoes, to see through their eyes, that's how peace begins. And it's up to you to make that happen. Empathy is a quality of character that can change the world." President

---

Writing for Rights, pages 161–163.
Copyright © 2025 *Patrice W. Glenn*
Published under exclusive licence by Emerald Publishing Limited
ISBNs: 978-1-83708-490-6 HB, 978-1-83708-491-3 PB,
978-1-83708-492-0 EPDF, 978-1-83708-493-7 EPUB

Obama's words emphasize empathy's role as the glue that holds societies together; empathy fosters compassion, unity, and kindness. However, if we take a moment to examine our current landscape, empathy often seems like an endangered species.

One need not look far to witness the repercussions of this empathy deficit. In our increasingly polarized world, we've become skilled at shouting across ideological divides but woefully inadequate at listening. We label those with differing opinions as adversaries rather than fellow humans with unique experiences, perspectives, and stories. Our public discourse has transformed into a battleground where empathy is seen as a sign of weakness, rather than a cornerstone of a civilized society.

The divisiveness and toxic culture are amplified by political strife and pride-inflated discord. Now, more than any previous period, the lines of blue and red, Democrat and Republication, donkey and elephant extend beyond liberal versus conservative ideologies or community and social responsibility versus individual rights and justice. Instead, healthy debates to arrive at more comprehensive decision-making have been swapped for personal attacks and the capacity to remain in power.

Social media, a double-edged sword of connectivity, has amplified this problem. It has become a platform where empathy can be drowned out by echo chambers and vitriol. Keyboard warriors, shielded by anonymity, often unleash hurtful words they would never dare to speak in person. Instead of understanding, we have become quick to judge, hasty to dismiss, and swift to forget the human being behind the screen.

The consequences of this empathy deficit are far-reaching. This gap erodes our relationships, polarizes our communities, and stymies our progress. It perpetuates discrimination, fuels injustice, and leaves countless voices unheard. It is a gaping wound in the fabric of our society, and its effects are acutely felt by the most vulnerable among us.

What can we do? The first step is to acknowledge that empathy is not a sign of weakness but a testament to our collective humanity. Empathy is a skill that can be cultivated and nurtured through active listening, open mindedness, and a willingness to engage with diverse perspectives. Henry Ford expressed his perception about empathy. He said, "If there is any one secret of success, it lies in the ability to get the other person's point of view and see things from his angle as well as your own." Empathy begins with seeing others as complex, flawed, and beautiful beings, just like ourselves.

It is time to turn down the volume on our own convictions for a moment and truly listen to the stories and struggles of those around us. It is time to extend a hand instead of pointing a finger. It is time to bridge divides with empathy, recognizing that our shared humanity is stronger than our differences.

In a world that often feels divided and disheartening, empathy is the beacon of hope we so desperately need. It is not a utopian ideal but a practical solution to healing our society's wounds. It is the key to building bridges, mending rifts, and creating a more compassionate and just world for everyone.

We cannot be remembered as the generation that allowed empathy to wither away. Instead, let us be the architects of a society where empathy is not a rare gem but a common thread that binds us all. Our future depends on it, and the time to act is now.

AUTHOR BIOGRAPHY

Patrice W. Glenn Jones is the Executive Director of Online Education and Programs at Alabama State University and a visiting scholar at Rutgers University Graduate School of Education. Patrice also holds instructional roles at Delaware State University and Widener University. This now virtual learning specialist began her career as an English teacher and radio air personality in Jacksonville, Florida, and she emphasizes her role as a "forever teacher" no matter the modality. In addition to being a champion of online teaching and learning, Patrice advocates for learning experiences that consider the whole student, are critical, immersed in the "real world," engaging, and culturally responsive. She also asserts that in far too many instances, education has lost its "feeling," and that learning can and should incorporate "fun". This former assistant professor, program director, educational consultant, and assistant dean is also an editor and writing mentor. Patrice has publications with The Journal of Negro Education, International Journal of Teacher Education and Professional Development, Samuel DeWitt Proctor Institute, Nova Science Publications, IAP Press, McFarland, Lexington Books, and more. Her work has been featured as editorials in Diverse Issues in Higher Education and Insider Higher Ed. She holds a PhD in educational leadership from Florida A&M University, a specialist degree in information science and learning technology from the University of Missouri-Columbia, and a master's degree, as well as a bachelor's degree, in English from the University of North Florida.